The
Garland Library
of
War and Peace

The
Garland Library
of
War and Peace

Under the General Editorship of

Blanche Wiesen Cook, *John Jay College, C.U.N.Y.*

Sandi E. Cooper, *Richmond College, C.U.N.Y.*

Charles Chatfield, *Wittenberg University*

Peace Projects
of the Seventeenth Century

comprising

Sully's Grand Design of Henry IV

from the Memoirs of

Maximilien de Béthune, duc de Sully

with an introduction by
David Ogg

The Law of War and Peace

Selections from

De Jure Belli ac Pacis

by

Hugo Grotius

translated, with an introduction, by
W. S. M. Knight

An Essay towards the Present
and Future Peace of Europe

by

William Penn

with a new introduction
for the Garland Edition by

J. R. Jacob and M. C. Jacob

Garland Publishing, Inc., New York & London
1972

The new introduction for this

Garland Library Edition is Copyright © 1972, by

Garland Publishing Inc.

———

All Rights Reserved

———

Library of Congress Cataloging in Publication Data
Main entry under title:

Peace projects of the seventeenth century.

(The Garland library of war and peace)
"Comprising Sully's Grand design of Henry IV from
the Memoirs of Maximilien de Béthune, duc de Sully,
with an introduction by David Ogg. The law of war and
peace, selections from De jure belli ac pacis, by Hugo
Grotius, translated, with an introduction, by W. S. M.
Knight. An essay towards the present and future peace
of Europe, by William Penn."
Includes bibliographies.
1. Peace. 2. International relations. 3. International law. I. Sully, Maximilien de Béthune, duc de,
1559-1641. Mémoires. English. Chapter 30. 1972.
II. Grotius, Hugo, 1583-1645. De jure belli et pacis.
English. Selections. 1972. III. Penn, William,
1644-1718. An essay towards the present and future
peace of Europe. 1972. IV. Series.
JX1945.P27   327'.172   79-147416
ISBN 0-8240-0214-8

Printed in the United States of America

Introduction

In the twentieth century we can justly feel an affinity for those of the seventeenth century who have experienced some of the worst wars in human history. Not until World Wars I and II did the destruction of people and land in Europe exceed that experienced by Germany during the Thirty Years' War. Like our predecessors of that century we have burned and maimed believers with whom we disagree not about religious concepts or practices but about social and political ideology. The difference between napalm and the stake is primarily technological. Of course then as now statesmen, philosophers, and religious leaders talked of peace, and the more inventive of them sought formulae — philosophical or political — by which peace might be secured. Three of their proposals, chosen for the insight they give us into the seventeenth century, are reprinted in this volume.

Each in its way deals with the central question of seventeenth century political theory: the means by which the needs and desires of self-interest could be rationalized. War served those needs; to the victor it brought power, the power to control trade routes, enlarge boundaries or to win souls. Material and spiritual victories were equally an expression of

5

*self-interest, and theorists assumed that interests had
to be gratified. They further postulated the existence
of a natural order governed by divinely sanctioned
natural laws. But war threatened the harmony and
stability ordained by God, and consequently the
aggressive expression of self-interest had to be
controlled. Not by denying powerful men the
enjoyment of their power, but by channeling their
power into the peaceful pursuit of self-interest would
seventeenth century theorists arrive at a workable
formula for peace. Each of the proposals in this
volume illustrates one or another version of their
assumption.*

    *Maximilian of Béthune, Duke of Sully (1559-
1641), was the chief minister of Henry IV of France
until his assassination in 1610.[1] Afterwards Sully
withdrew from state affairs and wrote his Memoirs of
which "the Grand Design of Henry IV" reprinted
here is a part. The work purports to be an account of
a scheme devised by the King to bring universal
peace. In truth Sully's treatment is a mixture of fact
and fiction. Henry IV did design to reduce Hapsburg
power by building an alliance system and imagined
that if it were successful he would become, in place
of the House of Austria, the arbiter of European
politics. But he never carried his plans as far as Sully
claims he did. To this extent the "Design" is Sully's,
and much of the evidence he supplied in attributing it
to his master was fabricated. But not until the late
nineteenth century was the deception exposed.[2] In*

the seventeenth and eighteenth centuries, therefore, Sully's rendering was read not as the speculations of an aged royal servant in retirement but as the program of one of the greatest monarchs of France in the full vigor of his years who might have carried it through to success but for the assassin's knife — and as such was that much more influential.

The King's design or not, Sully's account was nothing if not politic. Peace would come through a federation of European powers. The impetus would be material interest. The Hapsburgs were to be divested of all holdings in Europe save Spain and the islands of the Mediterranean. Other European states would receive the former Hapsburg lands in return for joining the federation. The Spanish empire was to be guaranteed in the possession of its territories overseas but would have to open them up to free trade with the rest of Europe. The Hapsburgs would have no alternative but to acquiesce in the dismemberment of their empire because effective resistance would be impossible when every state in Europe stood to gain at their expense.

Sully saw Christianity as constituting a menace to peace and suggested how it could be neutralized as an issue. First the governments of Europe were to settle the religion of their states once and for all. The rulers would have to decide between Catholicism, Lutheranism, and Calvinism, and those whose faith was different from that of their state would be coerced into exile. This amounted to a Peace of Augsburg —

INTRODUCTION

*with the addition of Calvinism as an option —
extended to the whole of Europe. Second the only
positive part religion was to play in binding Europe
together was the crusade Sully called for against the
Turk. Even here there was a material inducement in
the prospect of spoils. Furthermore, the use of the
federal army would divert Christians from warring
among themselves — a not untimely point in the early
years of the Thirty Years' War when the final
revisions of Sully's account were written. By the
crusade religious war would be removed beyond the
boundaries of Europe, and religion would thus be
made to neutralize itself as a factor making for war
within Europe.*

    *Hugo Grotius (1583-1645) was Dutch, a native of
the province of Holland, and a leading political figure
until he was thrown out of office and imprisoned in
1618 for having participated in the Remonstrant
revolt led by Jan van Oldenbarnevelt and put down
by Maurice of Nassau, William the Silent's son and
successor as Stadholder of Holland.*[3] *By 1621 Grotius
had escaped and fled to Paris where he was to live for
most of the rest of his life. There he went on with his
writing and found employment as a diplomat,
ultimately becoming Swedish Ambassador in France
from 1635 until his recall a few months before his
death.*[4] *In 1623 and 1624 he wrote* De Jure Belli ac
Pacis, *first published in Frankfurt in 1625, part of
which is reprinted here.*

    Like Sully, Grotius was a practical man of affairs.

8

But he was also a legal and religious scholar, and this made a difference to his thought. Unlike Sully, he did not foresee an end to war in Europe. Instead he constructed a theoretical framework which, if applied to politics, would limit the number and scope of wars. Hence the title of his work.

Basic to this framework are two ideas: natural law and divine providence. Providence of course refers to God's personal government of the universe and of man. By natural law Grotius means those precepts discoverable by human reason for the proper ordering of human conduct. According to Grotius, both ideas point to the same morality for the regulation of international affairs. Natural law tells man that he is not, as some would have it, a creature driven on by unrestrained self-interest. If this were so, endless war would be inevitable, and it would be folly to try to alter the situation. Fortunately this is not the case. Man's true nature is sociable and reasonable. Through his reasonableness he can be made to see that his real interests are served not by the reckless pursuit of self-interest but by self-restraint. This is true both for individuals living within a single state and for states in their relations with one another.[5] The rewards will follow — the benefits of a peaceful society in this life and salvation hereafter. As man realizes his true worldly interests, he is redeemed in the eyes of God. For Grotius God's providential order and the proper human order arrived at by man's application of natural law to human affairs are one. This identity is

9

expressed in other ways in Grotius' treatise. Christian charity, for instance, dictates that in war a victor show clemency. His long-term interests dictate the same because a harsh peace breeds fresh hostility. Just as the pursuit of true interest is the road to salvation in the next world, Christian charity smooths the way to the realization of long-term interests in this world. Christian piety and the rules of war and peace are the same, so men and states are obliged on two counts to bring their affairs into harmony with the rational dictates of natural law. Grotius was a leader of the Remonstrants in Holland, that faction within the Dutch Reformed Church who, adopting the ideas of Jacobus Arminius, rejected predestination and held man responsible for working out his own salvation. This Arminian sentiment is implicit in Grotius' treatise.[6]

In appealing to natural law as the means of regulating affairs between states, Grotius was reacting against two other conceptions of international relations current at the time — religious pacifism and the doctrine of raison d'état. *Contrary to the latter, he held that international politics are not synonymous with power politics; that there is a morality involved, namely, that of natural law, and hence that states cannot justify going to war from calculations of advantage.*[7] *But contrary to both the practitioners of power politics and the religious pacifists, he developed the concept of the just war. The power politicians did not admit considerations of justice into their calculus, and on religious grounds the pacifists did not believe in war.*[8] *Grotius held, however, that when the law of nature is violated by one state, other states are obligated to make war on the criminal. In such a case war becomes necessary and so legal, just and Christian. War is lawful where it is a matter (1) of a defense against injury, (2) of the recovery of what is legally due, or (3) of the punishment by third parties of a criminal aggressor against a state helpless in its own defense. This third legitimate rationale for war is "the first authoritative statement of the principle of humanitarian intervention" and as such is a remote ancestor of the Charter of the United Nations.*[9]

Apart from his notion of humanitarian intervention, what is the significance of Grotius' work in the history of proposals for peace? Did he, as many have claimed, emancipate international law from theology? Obviously he did not; for him, as we have shown, natural law was virtually another word for divine providence. But in linking Providence with the law of nature, self-interest, and state interest with irenical religion, he helped keep alive the tradition of religious humanism stemming from Erasmus, another Dutchman, and made an important contribution to the development of that most characteristic doctrine of the next century, enlightened interest. Besides his part in the creation of a new Christianity, a religion of worldly interest, Grotius' impact is due to one other factor. His conception of international relations resting upon a foundation of natural law is not original. The idea of the just war can be traced at least to St. Augustine. Grotius himself freely acknowledged his debt to his sixteenth and seventeenth century precursors, especially Francisco Suarez and Alberico Gentile.[10] *But we read him and not them because he was the first to attempt the treatment of the subject in its entirety.*

The sinews of Sully's peace are material interests, not religious ones. For Grotius religion and worldly interests, properly conceived, are one, and a combination of religious and material motives is what induces men to obey the laws of war and peace. Grotius is not neglecting Sully's material motives; by fusing them with religion, he spiritualizes them.

As a theoretician of peace Grotius commands the most philosophical interest of any of the three writers presented in this edition. Yet Sully was probably as influential. Certainly William Penn knew his scheme and appears to have been impressed by it.[11] *He shared Sully's fear and dislike of the Turks; although as a more consistent thinker, Penn was not willing to use war against them as a device for maintaining European peace.*

Not that peace was any less urgent a matter in Penn's time. When William Penn (1644-1718) wrote An Essay towards the Past and Future Peace of Europe *(1693) most of Europe was engaged in a war brought about by the territorial ambitions of France and the commercial rivalries of the three major powers, France, the Netherlands, and England. The English and the Dutch were allied in the League of Augsburg for the purpose of curtailing French encroachments on the territory of the Holy Roman Empire, and in turn they desired to secure their mercantile interests at the expense of France.*[12] *Furthermore English and Dutch propagandists, urged on by French Protestant refugees, claimed that they represented the cause of European Protestantism in its travail against the anti-Christ, the beast of the Roman Empire neatly personified by the French King, Louis XIV. Among some Protestants fervor for the war reached almost hysterical proportions — one French exile, Pierre Jurieu, combined espionage activities on behalf of his English allies with the publication of long treatises about the coming millennium and reign of the saints. War against France, he argued, had been predicted by the Scripture prophecies as yet another step in the struggle with anti-Christ. Each step brought victory closer. Finally the beast would be slain, Christ would come again to judge the wicked and institute a millennial paradise.*[13]

Jurieu's assessment of the righteousness of the Protestant cause conformed to the wishful thinking of some English bishops who also used Scripture to predict French defeat.[14] *Even those Continental Protestants, such as Pierre Bayle, who were sceptical about the uses to which Scripture could or should be put, nevertheless longed to see the French humiliated.*

INTRODUCTION

Many French Protestants had suffered exile or imprisonment when in 1685 Louis XIV revoked the Edict of Nantes and offered the Huguenots the choice of conversion to Catholicism or persecution. Their dispersion into the Netherlands, Geneva and England exacerbated hatreds as old as the Reformation itself. More crucial to English Protestants, however, was the accession in 1685 of a Catholic, James II, to the throne of England. Almost immediately he embarked on a plan to dismantle Anglican political and religious hegemony by installing Catholics in positions of leadership in the army, government and universities. At the same time he claimed only to seek religious toleration for his non-Anglican subjects, both Catholic and Protestant.

Opposition to his efforts grew and in November, 1688, William of Orange, the King's son-in-law and leader of the Dutch republic, invaded England at the invitation of a conspiratorial group of disaffected gentlemen and nobles. James II fled to France and William secured his revolution by having himself and his wife, Mary, declared King and Queen by act of parliament. William was now able to launch a war against France, its timing necessitated by the French invasion of Germany during the summer of 1688. The War of the League of Augsburg (1688-1697), as it is commonly called, began for William on two fronts, first in Ireland where James II's invasion had to be thwarted and then, after success in Ireland, on the Continent. America eventually became a battlefield as

INTRODUCTION

well, and only after a famine in France and financial exhaustion among the allies did peace result. The French were contained, and English and Dutch commercial interests were favored by the peace settlement.

In a war sanctioned by religious beliefs and hostilities it is perhaps surprising to find William Penn, the leading spokesman of the Quakers, proposing at its height a plan by which European peace might be secured, not just temporarily but permanently. The Protestant sect to which Penn gave his whole-hearted dedication belonged to the radical wing of the Reformation. Led by George Fox, the Quakers as they came to be called, arose in England during the civil wars of the 1640s. Inspired by their literal reading of scripture, the Quakers eschewed churches and churchmen as worldly corruptions designed to snare the unsuspecting Protestant. Only the Word revealed in Scripture and through the "inner light" communicated directly by God to the saints is necessary for salvation. The Quakers renounced politics and war and sought an inner reformation, one that would find them prepared to accept and be judged by Christ at his second coming, an event they were sure would be imminent. Indeed the early millenarianism of the Quakers closely resembles the millenarianism found among later French Protestants. Why then did Penn refuse to make common cause with them against anti-Christ? Even if the Quakers would not engage in military actions, Penn could have lent his authority in support of English and Dutch objectives.

Many factors went into making Penn's peace proposal. Although a close friend of George Fox and the other founders of the Quaker movement, William Penn represents the second generation of English Quakers. His conversion to Quakerism occurred after the Restoration, when the sect was regarded as an illegal organization and more importantly, after the Quakers had renounced their social and political militancy. During the turbulent 1650s their leaders had flirted with such political radicals as Sir Henry Vane. The Quakers had hoped to institute a social order that would bring justice to the economically disadvantaged, members of the lesser gentry, yeomanry and artisan communities, many of whom had become Quakers.[15] *But their efforts met with failure and after the Restoration, Quaker disillusionment unhinged their dreams of a millennial paradise to be instituted on earth. The Quakers turned inward, into a spiritual world that offered peace and divine comfort. For some this disillusionment with the social and political order meant emigration to a new world where another kind of paradise, characterized by religious liberty and prosperity, might be possible.*

Although a country gentleman of some substance, William Penn became one of those emigrants. After periodic imprisonment in the Tower for his heretical views, Penn went to America and through his friendship with the Duke of York, James II after

INTRODUCTION

1685, Penn secured a charter for a new colony. Although hardly the millennial paradise, Pennsylvania prospered and Penn became its first governor and its main defender and lobbyist in England. In that capacity he spent much of his time in London securing the colony's commercial and political interests. At court and in parliament Penn practiced the political art that his Quaker predecessors had abandoned, and he did it with some success. Only after the Revolution of 1688-89 did his fortunes change for a time. His close association with the dethroned monarch made him suspect of treason, and the war with France compounded his difficulties.[16]

In terms of mercantilist philosophy the colonies were meant to exist to further the prosperity of the mother country, not to compete with it. The activities of the Pennsylvanians had bothered English merchants for some time. But in the early 1690s English commerce suffered under the impact of the war. Most traders, however, blamed their hardships on the colonies; after all the war was meant to secure, not harm, English interests. Penn and his interests were a logical target for their annoyance. The merchants demanded controls and restrictions on the commercial activities of the colonies, and in 1696 they got their way by the passage of the Navigation Act. Although the merchants by and large supported the war, other powerful elements in English society opposed it. The less prosperous elements of the

17

landowning classes wanted an end to the war and its concomitant taxation burden. In the early 1690s they mounted considerable parliamentary opposition against the long-term funding of William's wartime expenses, and managed for a time to hold him to piecemeal subsidies.[17]

It is in this context of colonial commercial rights and country opposition that Penn's peace proposals assume significance in their own time. This is not to say that Penn's pacifism, based firmly on his religious convictions, can be dismissed as the machinations of a political lobbyist. On the contrary, Penn and his fellow Quakers deeply abhorred war and genuinely sought peace — even with France. But the arguments Penn presents in the following treatise were conditioned by his circumstances, by the political quietism of this second generation of Quakers, by his desire to secure the commercial interests of Pennsylvania, and by his politically astute attempt to appeal to the perhaps less altruistic anti-war sentiments of the country gentry. His proposal, he tells his readers, will have to suffice "till the Millenary Doctrine be accomplished, [for] there is nothing appears to me so beneficial an expedient to the Peace and Happiness of this Quarter of the World." Pragmatically Penn argues that war is expensive, and that it impairs commerce — a lesson he wanted English merchants to learn.

18

INTRODUCTION

Ultimately, however, it is Penn's religious convictions that determine his attitude toward war. War springs not from economic and political rivalries, although they play their part, but from the very corruption of men. War is an expression of our sinfulness and when fought by Christians it makes mockery of their beliefs. As an alternative to war, Penn proposes a European parliament where differences will be settled by debate and compromise, in effect by a "European League or Confederacy." Penn's treatise was one of the first attempts to work out a system for the maintenance of international peace similar to that eventually established by the League of Nations. But Penn does not stop there; he would channel human aggression into socially useful directions. In a Baconian spirit Penn proposes that men busy themselves with the study of nature for this gives "Men an Understanding of themselves, of the World they are born into, how to be useful and serviceable, both to themselves and others. . . ."

In the treatise that follows Penn has succeeded in channeling the millenarian dreams of the seventeenth century into a series of concrete proposals for the maintenance of peace and prosperity in our world. Penn failed to see that the very means by which this prosperity is attained by some lead inevitably to wars with others. His failure stems from his economic and political involvement in a commercial and imperialist system with the potential for unleashing aggression

INTRODUCTION

on a scale that men in the late seventeenth century could hardly have imagined.

J. R. Jacob
John Jay College—C.U.N.Y.

M. C. Jacob
Baruch College—C.U.N.Y.

INTRODUCTION

NOTES

[1] D. Buisseret, Sully, *1968*.

[2] C. Pfister, *"Les Economies Royales de Sully,"* Revue Historique, *1894, LIV-LVI.*

[3] P. Geyl, The Netherlands in the Seventeenth Century, *1961, I.*

[4] R. Warden Lee, *"Grotius — the Last Phase, 1635-1645,"* The Grotius Society, Transactions, *XXXI, 1945, pp. 211-212.*

[5] C. van Vollenhoven, *"The Framework of Grotius Book* De Jure Belli ac Pacis," Verhandelingen der Koninlijke Akademie van Wetenschappen to Amsterdam, *Afdeeling Letterkunde, Nieuwe Reeks, Deel XXX, No. 4, 1932, p. 14.*

[6] G. L. Mosse, *"Changes in Religious Thought," in* The New Cambridge Modern History, ed. J. P. Cooper, *1970, IV, pp. 169-201; and* R. Mousnier, *"The Exponents and Critics of Absolutism,"* ibid. pp. 111-112.

[7] Sir Hersch Lauterpacht, *"The Grotian Tradition in International Law,"* The British Year Book of International Law, *XXIII, 1946, pp. 30-35, 38.*

[8] C. van Vollenhoven, *"Grotius and the Study of Law,"* The American Journal of International Law, *XIX, 1925, p. 3.*

[9] Lauterpacht, op. cit., *p. 46.*

[10] Ibid., *pp. 8, 17, 36-37;* R. W. Lee, *"Hugo Grotius,"* Proceedings of the British Academy, *XVI, 1930, p. 276; and,* Gezina van der Molen, Alberico Gentili and the Development of International Law, *2nd ed. rev., Leyden, 1968, pp. 134-137.*

[11] Edward C. Beatty, William Penn as Social Philosopher, *New York, 1939, p. 100.*

[12] For an excellent account of the war see Sir George Clark, *"The Nine Years War, 1688-1697" in* The New Cambridge Modern History, *VI, 1970, pp. 223-253.*

[13] See The Accomplishment of the Scripture Prophecies, or the Approaching Deliverance of the Church, *London, 1687; also* G. H.

NOTES

Dodge, The Political Theory of the Huguenots of the Dispersion, *New York, 1947, and Walter Rex,* Essays on Pierre Bayle and Religious Controversy, *The Hague, 1965, pp. 197-255.*

[14]*E. de Beer, ed.,* The Diary of John Evelyn, *London, 1955, IV, p. 636; A. Tindal Hart,* William Lloyd, *London, 1952, p. 137; and again, Evelyn, V, pp. 25-26. For the War of Spanish Succession see Edward Fowler,* A Sermon Preached in the Chapel at Guildhall . . . , *London, 1704.*

[15]*James F. Maclear, "Quakerism and the End of the Interregnum: A Chapter in the Domestication of Radical Puritanism,"* Church History, *XIX, 1950, pp. 240-270. For a more adequate discussion of the social composition of the Quaker movement, see Richard T. Vann,* The Social Development of English Quakerism, *1655-1755, Cambridge, Mass. 1969.*

[16]*Joseph E. Illick,* William Penn the Politician, *Ithaca, New York, 1965.*

[17]*Dennis Rubini,* Court and Country, *1688-1702, London, 1967, pp. 79-81.*

THE GROTIUS SOCIETY PUBLICATIONS.

Texts for Students of International Relations.

No. 2.

SULLY'S
Grand Design of Henry IV.

FROM THE

Memoirs of Maximilien de Béthune duc de Sully (1559=1641).

WITH AN INTRODUCTION

·BY

DAVID OGG,

Fellow and Tutor of New College, Oxford.

Price 2/6 net.

SWEET AND MAXWELL, LIMITED,

3 CHANCERY LANE, LONDON, W.C. 2.

1921.

PRINTED AT READING, ENGLAND,
BY
THE EASTERN PRESS, LTD.

THE GRAND DESIGN OF HENRY IV.

INTRODUCTION.

Schemes for securing perpetual peace generally have for their
authors either philosophers (such as Bentham and Kant) or
accomplished scholars (like Pope Leo X.) or idealist statesmen
(*e.g.*, President Wilson), but rarely financiers.   The realm of
finance is an uncongenial one for the altruist and the day-dreamer;
the uncompromising, the matter-of-fact, and, perhaps, the un-
exuberant are likely to be its most flourishing types.   There is,
however, one striking exception to this generalisation.   Maximilian
of Béthune, Duke of Sully (1559—1641), acquired considerable
reputation as Henry IV.'s Superintendent of Finance after he had
laid the foundations of a very large private fortune from booty
appropriated in the troublous times preceding the accession of his
royal master.   His task as finance minister was a herculean one,
since not only had he to find new sources of revenue, increase the
prosperity of France by devising new roads and canals, and
redeem many Crown lands and prerogatives from pawn, but he
had also to reorganise the whole system of tax-collecting and,
perhaps most difficult of all, to refuse all grants of money to the
monarch that were likely to be spent in private pleasure.   That
imagination was not Sully's strongest characteristic is shown by
the fact that he was the first Chancellor of the Exchequer who
could boast that his budgets were honest.   Avarice, austerity, and
shrewdness were the qualities attributed to him by contemporaries; and in his Memoirs he shows that he was quite
aware of his reputation.   It is therefore a remarkable fact that
he should himself have been the author of one of the most
imaginative and comprehensive schemes for securing what so

-many have regarded as a mere chimera; and it is perhaps
evidence of his consciousness of this seeming inconsistency that
he took great pains to father the scheme on someone else.

Before examining the Grand Design in detail, it is necessary to
say something of the history of the book, a part of which is here
reprinted.

After the murder of Henry IV., Sully went into retirement;
and though during the minority. of Louis XIII. there were
a few occasions when he might have been invited to return
to public life, he was nevertheless condemned to political
inactivity for over thirty years. Like St. Simon after him, he
employed a considerable part of his enforced leisure in compiling
his Memoirs, and, like St. Simon also, he adopted a consistent
attitude of "laudator temporis acti." He had always prided
himself on his literary skill. During the lifetime of Henry he had
completed a biography of that monarch, and in retirement he
wrote several treatises on miscellaneous subjects. With the aid
of one of his secretaries, he began, about 1611, to draw up his
Memoires, or *Oeconomies Royales d'Estat*, and these were
at first compiled in the second person, the secretary calling to
mind the many achievements of Sully's administration. In this,
the original form, they were completed by about 1617, and the
manuscripts were acquired by the Bibliothèque Nationale in 1843.
These manuscripts contain six or seven references to what has
been called the Grand Design, and a brief enumeration of these
will reveal the scheme in embryo (a).

The first reference is under the year 1596, just after the submission of D'Epernon and when Henry's victory over his enemies
of the League was practically complete. According to Sully, Henry
took him aside and confessed that he hoped God would enable him
to retake Navarre, that he would be granted a victory against the
King of Spain, that he might, in some way, surpass the deeds of
Don John of Austria, the victor of Lepanto, and that he might be
relieved of his wife. He referred also to two great projects which
he wished to put into execution before his death, but these are
not specified by his biographer. The next reference in the MSS.
is in connection with Sully's embassy to England in 1603, when

(a) For a complete examination of these MSS., see the articles by Pfister in
Revue Historique, 1894, Vols. LIV., LV., and LVI.

he was sent to congratulate James on his accession. On this occasion Henry is credited with telling his ambassador that he wished to ally with England, Venice, the Low Countries, the Protestant princes and towns of Germany against Spain, and that for this purpose he wished to effect a marriage alliance with England. Together with these public instructions, Sully, according to his own account, was given certain secret commissions, and, in particular, was to confer with the English king on the following proposals:—

1. France, England, and Holland to combine their naval forces and seize the Spanish Indies or some of the islands on the routes of the Spanish treasure fleets.

2. The Hapsburgs, by the pressure of a great European coalition, to be deprived of the Empire and reduced to Spain.

3. The rivers Meuse, Moselle, and Rhine to be seized so as to control the Low Countries.

With regard to the proposed coalition against the Hapsburgs, Sully notes that all the participants were to benefit territorially except France and England.

The third reference is in 1604, when Sully records that he refused Henry a grant of public money for his pleasures on the ground that every penny would be required for the Grand Design. In 1609 there is a further allusion to the scheme when, in compliance with a request for an inventory of fortresses and troops, Sully proposed that two objects of policy should be, first, to transfer the Empire to some family other than the Hapsburgs, and, second, to confine the Hapsburgs to Spain. When, in this year, the Cleves-Julich succession question became acute, Sully relates that he encouraged Henry to commence hostilities, the French king having now secured the alliance of Savoy, Venice, the German princes, and the Low Countries, and having at his disposal an army of 150,000 men. The last reference is in 1610, when Sully is asked to put his proposals on record. This he does by enumerating all the alliances already formed against Spain, and suggests a scheme for dividing captured territory among the allies when the Hapsburgs shall have met with their inevitable defeat.

Such is the account of the Grand Design as given by Sully

shortly after his retirement. As it stands, it contains several inconsistencies and inventions: in particular, the account of the embassy of 1603 is more imaginative than historical. The letters reproduced, in the manuscript edition, to authenticate this mission are fabrications (b), and the secret instructions never existed but in the mind of Sully. It will be noticed also that in this account responsibility for the scheme is at one time attributed to the monarch, at another time to the minister. But, on the whole, the scheme as thus evolved is not unhistorical. Henry IV. certainly did meditate great designs against the Hapsburgs: he was at pains to build up a system of European alliances, and had he been spared the knife of Ravaillac he might have lived to see the downfall of the Empire. There is indeed ample contemporary evidence that such a general policy was attributed to him. There exists in manuscript (c) an account of a conversation between Henry and Lesdiguières on October 17, 1609. In this account, Henry confessed that he still felt young, and that he hoped God would give him other ten years to complete his work. He compared himself to an architect who has laid the foundations and must leave to a successor the completion of the edifice. He wished the Dauphin to marry a daughter of the Duke of Lorraine and his eldest daughter to marry a prince of Savoy. To the idea of a Spanish marriage he declared himself resolutely opposed, believing that no marriage policy could ever remove the menace to France of Spanish ascendancy, since " the rise of the one must inevitably be the ruin of the other." Finally, he hoped for the day when there would be but one religion in France, though for the present he was content to use Protestants as well as Catholics. Numerous references of this kind are to be found in seventeenth-century books. The *Journal* of Bassompierre, the *Histoire Universelle* of Agrippa d'Aubigné, and the Memoirs attributed to Richelieu (d) and Fontenay-Mareuil (e) allude to

(b) This has been conclusively shown by the independent researches of Pfister and Kukelhaus.

(c) Affaires Etrangères France, 767, f. 5, quoted in Hanotaux, *Histoire du Cardinal de Richelieu*, Vol. I., p. 260.

(d) Richelieu, or the scribe employed to compile his *Mémoires*, notes that in 1610 Henry IV. was in his fifty-eighth year, and that his age was therefore the most serious obstacle to the Grand Design (Richelieu, *Mémoires*, ed. Michaud et Poujoulat, pp. 12—16).

(e) *Mémoires* (ed. Michaud et Poujoulat, pp. 9—12).

such designs and credit Henry IV. with the ambition of raising
France, on the ruins of the Hapsburg Empire, to a commanding
position in Europe. Matthieu, in his *Histoire de Henri IV.*
(1631) says of him: " Sans les infidelités françaises, il eust fait
une partie du monde français, comme Probus l'avait fait romain."
As thus stated, the Grand Design resolves itself into little
more than a historical truism. Ascendancy in the councils
of Europe had traditionally been associated with the country
which produced such monarchs as Philip Augustus, St. Louis,
Philip the Fair, and Louis XII., and the lead taken by
France in the Crusades had helped to confirm this political pre-
eminence. As early as the fourteenth century, a French jurist (*f*)
had affirmed that supremacy in the affairs of Europe belonged to
the French monarchy by a kind of natural right, " ex nativæ
pronitatis ad melius jure.": In the fifteenth century, George
Podiebrad, King of Bohemia (1420—1471), evolved a scheme for
maintaining European tranquillity (*g*), and addressed himself first
of all to the King of France, believing that his approval was the
chief preliminary requisite. for the success of such schemes. But
Louis XI was a poor patron, benefiting more by the strife of his
neighbours than by their concord. The years of anarchy and
dynastic war following on the reigns of Louis XII. and Francis I.
deprived French kings of their birthright. With the restoration
of France under the great king Henry IV., it was not unnatural
that the tradition should be revived.

In this revival, there was a recrudescence of the old crusading
spirit. French policy since the time of Francis I. had tended to
an alliance with the Turk, whose fleets frequently harried
Hapsburg possessions on the Mediterranean coasts, and for this
reason it is unlikely that Henry himself ever meditated any
serious designs against the Turks. But nevertheless he was
probably familiar with the plan for a crusade proposed in 1609 by
a Greek Minotto (*h*). During the minority of Louis XIII., such
proposals take a more concrete form. The Duke of Nevers,

(*f*) Jean of Jandun.
(*g*) The scheme was drawn up by Marini in *De Unione Christianorum contra
Turcas.* See Ter Meulen, *Der Gedanke der Internationalen Organisation,*
pp. 108—123.
(*h*) Cf. Zinkeisen, *Geschichte des Osmanischen Reiches,* III. 859.

induced by the promises of the Greeks, actually inaugurated such a crusade, with the help and good will of France, but the attempt proved abortive.   A French ambassador (i) in Constantinople compiled a *Short Discourse on the Surest Means of Ruining the Ottoman Empire*.   Father Joseph—Richelieu's understudy and prompter—meditated for long the project of expelling the Turks from Europe, and even composed a *Turciade*.   At the time when Sully was compiling his Memoirs, a crusade against the infidel was so far from being a fantastic scheme as to be almost a commonplace of politics.

If it be added that the career of Richelieu must have proved an inspiration to a man of Sully's type, we shall have completed our enumeration of the contemporary influences that are evident in the first and manuscript edition of the Memoirs.   Richelieu revived and amplified the policy of Henry IV., which had been set aside during the regency of Marie de Medicis.   Before his death in 1643, the prerogatives of the Empire had been considerably diminished, Spain had become almost isolated, the Hapsburgs were being forced back on their hereditary lands, and French gold was already corrupting the German princes, Protestant and Catholic alike.   In a measure it is true to say that the real Grand Design was the inspiration and achievement of Richelieu, and it is noteworthy that the later edition of Sully's Memoirs—the only edition that was printed—was prepared in the period between 1620 and 1635, when the career of the great minister was of surpassing interest to every patriotic Frenchman, and especially to one imbued, as was Sully, with the glorious traditions of the reign of Henry IV.

Thus, despite certain inaccuracies and inconsistencies, the original draft of Sully's Memoirs, so far from containing any fanciful scheme for remaking the map of Europe and introducing an era of perpetual peace, simply reflects the dynastic ambitions of the Bourbons as pursued by Henri IV. and Richelieu.   But after 1617 Sully returned to his memoir-writing and, whether because of impaired mental and moral powers or whether because events seemed to be leading to the complete victory of France, he made very important changes in the revised version.

(i) De Brèves, *Discours abrégé des asseurez moyens de ruiner la monarchie des princes ottomans* (n. d).

Imagination now freely supplements fact, documentary evidence is carefully forged wherever it might help to give an appearance of verisimilitude, and, quite unconscious of discrepancies and inconsistencies, a far more wonderful Grand Design is evolved. To complete the illusion, Henry IV. is declared its author as the scheme seems more befitting a great monarch than a cautious financier. It is this revised version that was printed (the first part in 1638, the second part in 1662), and one reason for Sully deciding to make this version public may have been his desire to be revenged on Scipion Dupleix, who, in his official history of Henry's reign, had carefully underestimated the part played by Sully. In these printed texts, the Grand Design appears only in scattered fragments, but, nevertheless, so fully and carefully were they " documented " that most contemporary readers were led to believe that Henry IV. really had entertained a scheme for securing the peace of Europe. The genuineness of the printed Memoirs was explicitly affirmed by Hardouin de Péréfixe in 1661 (k), and the only pre-nineteenth-century writers who expressed their doubts were Vittorio Siri (l) and St. Simon (m).

It is therefore hardly to be wondered at that in the eighteenth century—a period as uncritical as the seventeenth is pedantic—the Memoirs of Sully were accepted at their face value. Voltaire expressly commended the writings of Sully and Péréfixe as reliable accounts of Henry's reign (n). The Abbé de St. Pierre based his " Projet de Paix Perpetuelle " on the assumption that the Grand Design was authentic. The finishing touch was given in 1745, when the Abbé de l'Ecluse des Loges published a new edition of the Memoirs, in which all the scattered fragments relating to the Grand Design were collected together and put into one chapter at the end (numbered XXX.). In doing this, the Abbé was taking an unwarrantable liberty with his text, for Sully had never presented the scheme as a consistent whole; but undoubtedly this helped to popularise the supposed plan of a popular king. By 1778 this compilation had gone through five

(k) *Histoire du Roi Henri le Grand*, Amsterdam, 1661. p. 383.
(l) *Memorie Recondite* (1677), Vol. I., p. 29.   According to Siri, Sully's Memoirs are " sparse di chimere e inverisimili."
(m) *Parallèle des trois premiers rois Bourbons* (ed. Faugère. pp. 137—145).
(n) *Essai sur les mœurs et l'esprit des nations*, Chapter CLXXIV.

editions, and, as thus presented, the Grand Design was elevated
to the level of a philosophical system. Rousseau said that it
was not good enough for Europe, because Europe was not good
enough for it (o); and even Bentham may have been sub-
consciously influenced when he entrusted the inauguration of his
European fraternity of utilitarian States to the combined
influence of France and England. Echoes of Sully may be
detected here and there in Kant. The direct inspiration of
Sully can be traced in the peace projects of more obscure writers,
from the Englishman Bellers (p) and· the German Rachel (q) to
the Frenchman Saintard (r). The scheme attributed to Cardinal
Alberoni is little more than a plagiarism. Sully's "Grand Design"
is thus the starting-point of many of the schemes which have since
been put forward for establishing European peace, and this because
it was the first proposal, based on considerable knowledge of
European politics, which accepted facts and which presupposed
that peace may be not only a moral ideal but a practical blessing.
If States can no longer be influenced by religion, they may yet be
persuaded by political economy. That is the measure of Sully's
difference from his predecessors ·and the reason for his influence
in later times.

The Grand Design is based on two things—an acceptance, so
far as possible, of the *status quo*, and an appeal to the innate
selfishness of man. The three standard religions (Catholic,
Lutheran, and Calvinist) are admitted; the constitutional forms,
whether monarchical or republican, of the European States are
accepted as standards, and thus there is to be a minimum of
dislocation when Europe is united in the great federation of
hereditary monarchies, elective monarchies, and republics. There
is, moreover, evidence of some historical insight in the details of
the scheme. Holland and Switzerland are to be confirmed in their
republican traditions; Italy is to be freed from the foreigner.
The Pope is to become a secular prince—an intelligent apprecia-
tion of some later papal developments; and the Duchy of Savoy
is to be made a monarchy—perhaps the earliest anticipation of

(o) In his Essay on St. Pierre's *Projet de Paix Perpetuelle.*
(p) *Some reasons for an European State Proposed to the Powers of Europe,*
1710.
(q) *De Jure Naturæ et Gentium Dissertationes,* 1676.
(r) *Roman Politique sur l'état présent des affaires de l'Amerique,* 1757.

the great destiny in store for that house. Russia is considered as a power which might more legitimately develop in Asia than in Europe, and as, in any case, too risky a speculation for European investment. As intelligent knowledge of contemporary Europe is the basis of the scheme, so the inducement for prospective partners is one which even the most bellicose could scarcely refuse—the promise of additional territory, and this at the expense of the House of Austria. It does not occur to Sully that by dividing up Hapsburg territory he might create a permanent tradition of *revanche*. The military forces of this great European confederacy are to be directed to one object—the expulsion of the Turk from Europe.

Within this confederation there would be freedom of commerce, and supreme control would be vested in a senate of about sixty-six persons elected every three years from the participating States, a certain number of representatives being assigned to each. There would be subordinate and local assemblies: the decisions of the general senate only would be "final and irrevocable decrees." The Grand Design has for its backing a composite army, but whether this would be permanent and employed to enforce, if necessary, the decisions of the League, is not quite clear from the text.

Sully's preference for a city of Central Europe as the permanent seat of the senate's activities is noteworthy as, in some respects, an anticipation of the part to be played in later irenist ideals by the Germanic Confederation. Within a few years of his death, the League of the Rhine, in attempting to revive something of German nationalism, attempted also to create a guarantee for the peace of Europe by uniting (with German princes) that power which was most likely to have "annexationist" designs (at German expense), and whose ambitions might thus be neutralised by compact rather than by challenge. Throughout the eighteenth century, indeed, the very existence of the Germanic Confederation was regarded as making for European peace. Its geographical position was held to impose a restraint on ambitious neighbours, and at least one observer maintained that its weight secured that equilibrium to which, despite wars, Europe was (in this view) always automatically restored. It is not less noteworthy that,

of the German States, Prussia was considered the most important
as a model of good government and as the strongest rivet in this
great bulwark against anarchy and aggression. Mirabeau (s)
wrote: " Si la Prusse périt, l'art de gouverner retournera vers
l'enfance "; and his admiration was shared by French political
thinkers from Voltaire to Rousseau.

It is thus in its concreteness and in its anticipation of several
later doctrines of importance that Sully's Grand Design is of most
interest to the modern student of international relations. To
criticise it in points of detail would scarcely be fair, especially
as the scheme was only gradually evolved and was never reduced
by its author to a studied form. No doubt one of the weakest
parts of the Design is that the Senate—merely an echo of the
Imperial Diet—would lose its authority as soon as litigants found
that it was not in their interests to obey its behests, but the same
weakness may be detected in some more modern projects. Moreover, there is an appeal to base motives in the inception of the
scheme, the participants, with the possible exception of France
and England, being brought together by the promise of shares in
an Empire about to be dismembered. But Sully may have
regarded that as means to an end and, like a true optimist, he
may have hoped that once his League was established it would,
by a gradual and educative process, eliminate rapacity and
aggression from international politics. For it is Sully's greatest
merit that he preached certain truths, a respect for which in the
minds of responsible statesmen might have saved Europe from
many years of disaster and crime. Long before Montesquieu and
Rousseau this austere Huguenot proclaimed that the happiness
and success of a nation may be in inverse ratio to its territorial
extent (t), that wars of aggrandisement defeat their own object,
and that in great European struggles the plight of the victor may
be at least as unhappy as that of the conquered (u). Who can
say that these axioms have yet been understood by those who are

(s) In the conclusion to his *Monarchie Prussienne.*
(t) See *infra*, p. 24.
(u) Cf. Memoirs, Bk. IX. (1598). "I am not afraid to say that in the
present state of Europe it is almost equally unhappy for its princes to succeed
or miscarry in their enterprises, and that the true way of weakening a powerful
neighbour is not to carry off his spoils but to leave them to be shared by
others."

entrusted with the direction of international policy in Europe? Who can dispel from our minds the nightmare of a future world-war of *revanche* or territorial greed? Sully's Grand Design is unsound, unhistorical, and out-of-date, but it is because it has still some lessons for a world grown sick of war that its reprint here may be justified.

BIBLIOGRAPHY.

The text used in this reprint is that of the eighteenth-century English translation (6 vols., London, 1778, and Dublin, 1781). This text was reprinted with a few changes in Bohn's series (4 vols., 1892), and it should be noted that the chapter here reprinted (numbered XXX.) is the composite chapter first inserted by the Abbé de l'Ecluse des Loges in his edition of 1745. It is through this composite chapter that the Grand Design is most familiar to modern times, and so it has been reprinted here. A few minor changes have been made in the English version where it seemed obscure, even at the expense of giving a somewhat free translation of the original. The eighteenth-century footnotes (mostly valueless) have been omitted and a few elementary notes inserted in their place.

A. *Editions of the Memoirs.*

1. *Mémoires des sages et royales oeconomies d'Estat domestiques, politiques et militaires de Henry le Grand.* Vols. I. and II., (Chateau de Sully). 1638.
2. *Ibid.* Vols. III. and IV. Paris, 1662. Two volumes in one.
3. *Ibid.* 8 vols. Rouen, 1663.
4. *Ibid.* 4 vols. Paris, 1664.
5. *Mémoires de Maximilian de Béthune, duc de Sully . . . mis en ordre avec des remarques par M.L.D.L.D.L.* [Abbé de l'Ecluse des Loges.] London, 3 vols. (Subsequent editions in 1747 (3 vols.), 1752 (8 vols.), 1778 (10 vols.), and 1778 (revised, 8 vols.).
6. *Mémoires du Duc de Sully.* Paris, 1822. 6 vols.
7. *Mémoires des sages et royales oeconomies d'Estat, domestiques, politiques et militaires de Henry le Grand* (in Michaud et Poujoulat, "Nouvelle Collection des Mémoires pour servir à l'histoire de France," 2nd series, Vols. II. and III.). Paris, 1850.

B. *Monographs relating to the Grand Design.*

1. MORITZ RITTER.—*Die Memoiren Sullys und der grosse Plan Heinrichs IV.* (in Abhandlungen der historischen Classe der kgl. bayerischen Akademie der Wissenschaften. Bd. XI. Abth. III., 1870).

2. CORNELIUS.—*Der Grosse Plan Heinrichs IV. von Frankreich.* (" Münchener Historischer Jahrbuch," 1886).

3. T. KUKELHAUS.—*Der Ursprung des Planes vom ewigen Frieden.* Berlin, 1892.

4. C. PFISTER.—*Les Oeconomies Royales de Sully* (in " Revue Historique "). Vols. 54—56. 1894.

C. *General Works for Reference.*

1. LAVISSE.—*Histoire de France.* Vol. VI., Part 2.

2. HANOTAUX.—*Histoire du Cardinal de Richelieu.* 2 vols. 1893-6.

3. FAGNIEZ.—*Le Père Joseph et Richelieu.* 1894.

4. TER MEULEN.—*Der Gedanke der Internationalen Organisation.* 1917.

MEMOIRS OF THE DUKE OF SULLY.

BOOK XXX.

Wherein is discussed the Political Scheme,

commonly called

The Great Design of Henry IV.

As this part of these Memoirs will be chiefly taken up with an account of the great design of Henry IV. or the political scheme, by which he proposed to govern, not only France, but all Europe, it may not be improper to begin it with some general reflections on the French monarchy and on the Roman empire. We know that on the ruins of the Roman empire were formed not only the French but all the other powers comprising the Christian world.

If we consider all those successive changes which Rome has suffered from the year of its foundation, its infancy, youth and virility; its declension, fall and final ruin; these vicissitudes, which it experienced in common with the great monarchies by which it was preceded, would almost incline one to believe that empires, like all other sublunary things, are subject to be the sport and at last to sink under the pressure of time. Extending this idea still further, we perceive that all states are liable to be disturbed in their careers by certain extraordinary incidents which might be termed epidemic disorders. These frequently hasten the destruction of empires and, their cure by this discovery becoming easier, we may at least save some of them from catastrophes so fatal.

But if we endeavour to discover more visible and natural causes of the ruin of this vast and formidable empire, we shall perhaps soon perceive they were produced by a deviation from those wise laws and that simplicity of manners, which were the

origin of all its grandeur, into luxury, avarice and ambition.
Yet there was, finally, another cause, the effect of which could
hardly have been prevented or foreseen by the utmost human
wisdom; I mean, the irruptions of those vast bodies of barbarous
people, Goths, Vandals, Huns, Herulians, Rugians, Lombards,
&c. from whom, both separately and united, the Roman empire
received such violent shocks that it was at last overthrown by
them. Rome was three times sacked by these Barbarians; under
Honorius, by Alaric, chief of the Goths; by Genseric, king of the
Vandals, under Martin; and under Justinian, by Totila and the
Goths. Now if it be true that, after this, the city retained only
the shadow of what she had been; if we must regard her as
divested of the empire of the world, when her weakness and the
abuses of her government made her fall to be looked upon, not
simply as inevitable, but as very near, and, in fact, already
arrived; the date of her fall may then be marked long before the
reign of Valentinian III. to whom it will be doing a favour to
call him the last emperor of the West. For several of those
emperors whom he succeeded were, in reality, no better than
tyrants, by whom the empire was torn and divided, and the
shattered remnants left to be the spoil of the Barbarians, who,
indeed, by their conquests, acquired an equal right to them.

Rome, nevertheless, by intervals, beheld some faint appearances
of a revival; those of which she was most sensible were under
the reign of the great Constantine, whose victories once more
united this vast body under one head. But when he transported
the seat of his empire from Rome to Constantinople, he, by that
step, contributed more to the destruction of a work which had
cost him so much labour than all the ill conduct of his predecessors had been able to effect; and this even he rendered
irremediable, by dividing his empire equally between his three
sons. Theodosius, who by good fortune, or from his great valour,
found himself in the same circumstances with Constantine,
would not perhaps have committed the same fault, had he not
been influenced by the force of Constantine's example; but this
in a manner necessarily obliged him to divide his empire in two;
Arcadius had the East, Honorius the West: and from that time
there never were any hopes nor opportunity of reuniting them.

According to the order of nature, by which the destruction of one kingdom becomes the instrument for the production of others; so, in proportion as the most distant members of the empire of the East fell off from it, from thence there arose kingdoms; though indeed they did not at first bear that rank. The most ancient of these (its origin appearing to have been in the eighth year of the empire of Honorius) is undoubtedly that which was founded in Gaul by the French, so called from Franconia, from whence they were invited by the Gauls, inhabitants of the countries about the Moselle, to assist them in their deliverance from the oppression of the Roman armies. It being a custom among these Franks or French, to confer the title of king upon whatever person they chose to be their leader; if the first or second of these chiefs have not borne it, it is certain, at least, that the third, Merovius, and more particularly Clovis, who was the fifth, were invested with it. Some of them supported the royal title with so much glory, including Pepin and Charles Martel (to whom it would be doing an injustice to refuse this dignity), that their worthy successor Charlemagne, in Gaul, revived an imperfect image of the now extinguished empire in the West. This indeed was facilitated by those natural advantages France enjoys of numerous inhabitants trained to war and a great plenty of all things serving the different necessities of life, joined to a very great conveniency for commerce, arising from its situation, rendering it the centre of four of the principal powers of Europe; Germany, Italy, Spain, and Britain, with the Low Countries.

Let us here just say one word upon the three races which compose the succession of our kings: in the first of them I find only Merovius, Clovis I. and Clovis II.; Charles Martel, Pippin the Short, and Charlemagne in the second, who have raised themselves above the common level of their race. Take away these six from the thirty-five, which we compute in these two races, and all the rest, from their vices or their incapacity, appeared to have been either wicked kings, or but the shadow of kings; though among them we may distinguish some good qualities in Sigebert and Dagobert, and a very great devotion in Lewis the Debonnair, which, however, ended in his repenting the loss of empire and his kingdom, together with his liberty, in a cloister.

The Carlovingian race having reigned obscurely, the crown then descended upon a third (a); the four first kings of which, in my opinion, appear to have been perfect models of wise and good government. The kingdom which came under their dominion had lost much of its original splendour, for from its immense extent in the time of Charlemagne, it was reduced to nearly the same bounds which it has at .this day. There was this difference, however, that though these kings might have desired to restore the ancient limits of their territories, they had no means of doing so, since the form of government was such that the monarchs were subject to the great men of the realm who had a right to choose and even govern their sovereigns. The conduct therefore which they pursued was to condemn arbitrary power to an absolute silence; and, in its place, to substitute equity itself: a kind of dominion which never excites envy. Nothing now was done without the consent of the great men and the principal cities, and almost always in consequence of the decision of an assembly of the estates. A conduct so moderate and prudent put an end to all factions, and stifled all conspiracies, which are fatal to the state or the sovereign. Regularity, economy, a distinction of merit, strict observance of justice, all the virtues which we suppose necessary qualifications for the good of a family, were what characterized this new government, and produced what was never before beheld, and what perhaps we may never see again, an uninterrupted peace (b) for one hundred and twenty-two years. What the Capetians gained by this for themselves was the advantage of introducing into their house a hereditary right to the crown, and this could never have been procured for them by the sole authority of the Salic law. But they nevertheless thought it a necessary precaution not to declare their eldest sons for their successors till they had modestly asked the consent of the people, preceding it by a kind of election, usually having them crowned in their own life-time and seated with them upon the throne.

(a) That is, the Capetian race.
(b) The period between the accession of Hugh Capet (987) and that of Louis VI. (1108).

Philip II. whom Lewis VII. his father caused to be crowned, and reign with him in this manner was the first who neglected to observe this ceremony between the sovereign and his people. Several victories, obtained over his neighbours and subjects having gained him the surname of Augustus, served to open him a passage to absolute power, and a notion of the fitness and legality of this power, by the assistance of favourites, ministers and others, became afterwards so strongly imprinted in his successors, that they looked upon it as a mark of good policy to act contrary to those maxims, the general and particular utility of which had been so effectually confirmed by the experience of his predecessors. And this they did without any fear or perhaps without any conception of the fatal consequences which such a proceeding must necessarily incur at the hands of a nation which adores its liberty. This they might have deduced from the means to which the people had immediate recourse when they saw their liberties threatened. The kings could never obtain of their people any other than that kind of constrained obedience which always inclines them to embrace with eagerness all opportunities of mutiny. This was the source of a thousand bloody wars: that by which almost all France was ravaged by the English; that which we had with Italy, Burgundy, Spain. All of them can be attributed to no other causes than the civil dissensions by which they were preceded and here the weakest side, stifling the voice of honour, and the interest of the nation, constantly called in foreigners to assist them in the support of their tottering liberties. These were shameful and fatal remedies: but from that time they were constantly employed, down even to our times, by the house of Lorraine, in a league, for which religion was nothing more than the pretence (c). Another evil, which may at first appear to be of a different kind, but which, in my opinion, proceeds from the same source, was a general corruption of manners, a thirst for riches and a most shameful degree of

(c) Sully may here be thinking of the affair of the bishopric of Strasburg (1595). In that year Henry, as arbitrator, divided the episcopal domains between the Protestant Elector of Brandenburg and the Catholic Charles of Lorraine. The latter refused to adhere to this, and, by appointing as his coadjutor the Archduke Leopold, cousin of the Emperor Rudolph, was bidding for the support of France's enemy.

luxury: these, sometimes separately, and sometimes united, were alternate causes and effects of many of our miseries.

Thus, in a few words, I have exposed the various species of our bad policy with respect both to the form of the government, successively subjected to the will of the people, the soldiers, the nobles, the states and the kings, and in regard to the persons likewise of these last, whether dependent, elective, hereditary, or absolute.

From the picture here laid before us we may be enabled to form our judgment upon the third race of our kings: we may find a thousand things to admire in Philip Augustus, Saint-Lewis, Philip le Bel, Charles the Wise, Charles VII. and Lewis XII. But it is to be lamented that so many virtues or great qualities have been exercised upon no better principles; with what pleasure might we bestow upon them the titles of great kings, could we but conceal that their people were miserable: what might we not, in particular, say of Lewis IX.? Of the forty-four years which he reigned, the first twenty of them exhibit a scene not unworthy of comparison with the last eleven of Henry the Great. But I am afraid all their glory will appear to have been destroyed in the twenty-four following; wherein it appears that the excessive taxes upon the subjects, to satisfy an ill-judged and destructive devotion; immense sums transported into the most distant countries, for the ransom of prisoners; so many thousand subjects sacrificed; so many illustrious houses extinguished; caused a universal mourning throughout France, and altogether a general calamity.

Let us for once, if it is possible, fix our principles; and being, from long experience, convinced that the happiness of mankind can never arise from war (of which we ought to have been persuaded long ago), let us upon this principle take a cursory view of the history of our monarchy. We will pass by the wars of Clovis and his predecessors, because they seem to have been in some degree necessary to confirm the recent foundations of the monarchy: but what shall we say of those wars in which the four sons of Clovis, the four sons of Clotaire I. and their descendants were engaged, during the uninterrupted course of one hundred and sixty years? and of those also, by which, for the space of one hundred seventy-two other years, commencing with Lewis le Debonnaire, the kingdom was harassed and torn? What follows is still worse. The slightest knowledge of our history is sufficient to convince any one that there was no real tranquillity in the kingdom from Henry III. to the peace of Vervins : and, in short, all this long period may be called a war of nearly four hundred years' duration (d). After this examination (from whence it incontestibly appears that our kings have seldom thought of any thing but how to carry on their wars) we cannot but be scrupulous in bestowing on them the title of Truly Great kings; though we shall, nevertheless, render them all the justice which appears to have been their due. For I confess (as indeed it would be unjust to attribute to them alone, a crime which was properly that of all Europe) that several of these princes were sometimes in such circumstances as rendered the wars just, and even necessary : and from hence, when indeed there were no other means to obtain it, they acquired a true and lasting glory. Moreover, from the manner in which several of these wars were foreseen, prepared for and conducted, we may in their councils discover such master-strokes of policy, and in their persons such noble instances of courage, as are deserving of our highest praises. From whence then can proceed the error of so many exploits, in appearance so glorious, though the effect of them has generally been the devastation both of France and all Europe? I repeat it again, of all Europe, which even yet seems scarce sensible that in her present situation, a situation in which she has been for several centuries, every attempt tending to her subjection, or only to the too considerably augmenting of any one of her principal monarchies at the expense of the others, can never be any other than a chimerical and impossible enterprise. There are none of these monarchies but whose destruction would require a concurrence of causes infinitely superior to all human force. The whole, therefore, of what seems proper and necessary to be done, is to support them all in a kind of equilibrium; and whatever prince thinks, and in consequence acts otherwise, may indeed

(d) Including the twenty-two years between the accession of Henri III. and the Peace of Vervins, this gives a total period of 354 years.

cause torrents of blood to flow through all Europe, but he will
never be able to change her form.

When I observed that the extent of France is not now so
considerable as it was in the time of Charlemagne, my intention
was not that this diminution should be considered as a misfortune. In an age when we feel the sad effects of having had
ambitious princes for our kings, were all to concur in flattering
this fatal ambition, it would be the cause of still greater evils;
and it may be generally observed that the larger the extent of
kingdoms, the more they are subject to great revolutions and
misfortunes (e). The basis of the tranquillity of our own country,
in particular, depends upon preserving it within its present limits.
A climate, laws, manners, and language, different from our own;
seas, and chains of mountains almost inaccessible, are all so many
barriers, which we may consider as fixed even by nature. Besides,
what is it that France wants! will she not always be the richest
and most powerful kingdom in Europe? It must be granted.
All therefore which the French have to wish or desire is that
Heaven grant them pious, good, and wise kings; and that these
kings may employ their power in preserving the peace of Europe;
for no other enterprise can truly be to them either profitable or
successful.

And this explains to us the nature of the design which
Henry IV. was on the point of putting in execution when it
pleased God to take him to Himself, too soon by some years for
the happiness of the world. From hence likewise we may
perceive the motives of his pursuing a conduct so opposite to
any thing that had hitherto been undertaken by crowned heads:
and here we may behold what it was that acquired him the title
of Great. His designs were not inspired by a mean and despic-
able ambition, nor guided by base and partial interests: to render
France happy for ever was his desire, and she cannot perfectly
enjoy this felicity, unless all Europe likewise partake of it. So

---

(e) Cf. Montesquieu : " Si une république est petite, elle est détruite par une
force étrangère; si elle est grande, elle se détruit par une vice interieure "
(De l'Esprit des Lois. IX. 1): Rousseau : " De deux états qui nourrissent
le même nombre d'habitants, celui qui occupe une moindre étendue de terre est
réellement le plus puissant " (Projet de Paix Perpetuelle); and Volney :
" Ce sont les grands états qui ont perdu les mœurs et la liberté des peuples "
(Considerations sur la guerre actuelle des Turcs).

it was the happiness of Europe in general which he laboured to procure, and this in a manner so solid and durable, that nothing should afterwards be able to shake its foundations.

I must confess I am under some apprehensions, lest this scheme should at first be considered as one of those chimeras, or idle political speculations, in which a mind susceptible of strange and singular ideas may be so easily engaged. Those who shall thus think of it must be that sort of people on whom first impressions have the force of truth; or those, who by their distance from the times, and their ignorance of the circumstances, confound the wisest and noblest enterprises that have ever been formed, with those chimerical projects which princes, intoxicated with their power, have in all ages amused themselves in forming. I confess, that if we attentively examine the designs which have been planned from motives of vanity, confidence in good fortune, ignorance, nay, from sloth, and even timidity itself, we must be surprised at beholding sovereigns plunged blindly into schemes, specious perhaps in appearance, but which at bottom have not the least degree of possibility. The mind of man, with so much complacency, nay, even with so much ardour, pursues whatever it fancies great or beautiful that it is sorry to realise that these objects have frequently nothing real or solid in them. But in this, as well as in other things, there is an opposite extreme to be avoided; namely, that as we usually fail in the execution of great designs, from not commencing and continuing them with sufficient vigour and spirit, so likewise we are defective in the knowledge of their true worth and tendency, because we do not thoroughly and properly consider them in all their dependencies and consequences. I have myself been more difficult to persuade in this matter than perhaps any of those who shall read these Memoirs, and this I consider as an effect of that cold, cautious and unenterprising temper, which makes so considerable a part of my character.

I remember the first time the king spoke to me of a political system, by which all Europe might be regulated and governed as one great family, I scarce paid any attention to what he said, imagining that he meant no more by it than merely to divert himself, or perhaps to shew that his thoughts on political subjects

were greater and penetrated deeper than most others: and my
reply was a mixture of pleasantry and compliment. Henry said
no more at that time. He often confessed to me afterwards, that
he had long concealed from me what he meditated on this subject,
from a sense of shame, which many labour under, lest they should
disclose designs which might appear ridiculous or impossible. I
was astonished when, some time after, he renewed our conversation on this head and continued from year to year to entertain
me with new regulations and new improvements in this scheme.

I had been very far from thinking seriously about it. If by
accident it came into my thoughts for a moment, the first view
of the design, which conceived a re-union of all the different
states of Europe; immense expenses, at a time when France
could scarce supply her own necessities; a concatenation of
events, which to me appeared infinite : these were considerations
which had always made me reject the thought as vain. I even
apprehended there was some illusion in it, and I recollected some
of those enterprises in which we had endeavoured to engage
Europe. I considered those in particular which had been formed
by some of our kings, from much less considerable motives, and
I felt myself disgusted with this, from the bad success of all the
former. The disposition of the princes of Europe to take umbrage
against France, when she would have assisted them to dissipate
their fears from the too great power of Spain, this alone to me
appeared an unsurmountable obstacle.

Strongly prejudiced by this opinion, I used my utmost efforts
to undeceive Henry, who, on his side, surprised not to find me of
his sentiment in any one point, immediately undertook, and
readily succeeded in convincing me that my thus indiscriminately
condemning all parts of his project in which he was certain that
every thing at least was not blameable, could proceed from
nothing but strong prejudices. I could not refuse, at his solicita-
tions, to use my endeavours to gain a thorough comprehension
   it. I formed a clearer plan of it in my mind. I collected and
united all its different branches. I studied all its proportions and
dimensions, if I may say so, and I discovered in them a regularity
and mutual dependence, of which, when I had only considered
the design in a confused and careless manner, I had not been at

all sensible. The benefit which would manifestly arise from it to all Europe was what most immediately struck me, as being in effect the plainest and most evident; but the means to effect so good a design were, therefore, what I hesitated at the longest. The general situation of the affairs of Europe, and of our own in particular, appeared to me every way contrary to the realisation of the project. I did not consider that, since the execution of the scheme might be deferred till a proper opportunity, we could prepare ourselves with all those resources which time affords to those who know how to make the best use of it. I was at last convinced, that however disproportionate the means might appear to the effect, a course of years, during which every thing should as much as possible be made subservient to the great object in view, would surmount many difficulties. It is indeed somewhat extraordinary that this point, which appeared to be and really was the most difficult of any, should at last become the most easy.

Having thus seen all parts of the design in their just points of view, having thoroughly considered and calculated and from thence discovered and prepared for all events which might happen, I found myself confirmed in the opinion, that the design of Henry the Great was, upon the whole, just in its intention, possible and even practicable in all its parts, and infinitely glorious in all its effects. So that, upon all occasions, I was the first to recall the king to his engagements, and sometimes to convince him by those very arguments which he himself had taught me.

The constant attention this prince paid to all affairs transacted round him arising from those singularly unhappy circumstances by which, in almost every instant of his life, he found himself embarrassed, had been the cause of his forming this design even from the time when, being called to the crown by the death of Henry III. he considered the humbling of the house of Austria as absolutely necessary for his security. Yet, if he was a beholden to Elizabeth for his thought of the design, it is, however, certain that this great queen had herself conceived it long before, as a means to avenge Europe for the attempts of its common enemy. The troubles in which all the following years were engaged, the war which succeeded in 1595, and that against Savoy after the peace of Vervins, forced Henry into difficulties which obliged him to lay aside all thoughts of other affairs; and it was not till after his marriage and the firm re-establishment of peace, that he renewed his thoughts upon his first design, the execution of which appeared then more impossible, or at least more improbable, than ever.

He, nevertheless, communicated it by letters to Elizabeth, and this was what inspired them with so strong an inclination to confer together in 1601 when this princess came to Dover and Henry to Calais. What the ceremony of an interview would not have permitted them to do I at last begun by the voyage which I made to this princess. I found her deeply engaged in the means by which this great design might be successfully executed; and, notwithstanding the difficulties which she apprehended in its two principal points, namely, the agreement of religions and the equality of the powers, she did not to me appear at all to doubt of its success. This she chiefly expected, for a reason of the justness of which I have since been well convinced, namely, that as the plan was only contrary to the design of some princes, whose ambitious views were sufficiently known to all Europe, this fact would rather promote than retard its success. She farther said, that its execution by any other means than that of arms would be very desirable, as this has always something odious in it: but she confessed that indeed it would be hardly possible to begin it otherwise. A very great number of the articles, conditions, and different dispositions is due to this queen and sufficiently shew, that in respect of wisdom, penetration, and all the other perfections of the mind, she was not inferior to any king the most truly deserving of that title.

It must indeed be considered as a very great misfortune that Henry could not at this time second the intention of the queen of England, who wished to have the design put in immediate execution; but when he thus laid the foundation of the edifice he scarcely hoped to see the time when the finishing hand would be put to it. The recovery of his own kingdom from the various maladies by which it was afflicted was a work of several years; and unhappily he had himself seen forty-eight when he began it.

He pursued it, nevertheless, with the greatest vigour. The edict of Nantes had been published with this view and every other means was used which might gain the respect and confidence of the princes of Europe. Henry and I, at the same time, applied ourselves with indefatigable labour to regulate the interior affairs of the kingdom. We considered the death of the king of Spain (*f*) as the most favourable event that could happen to our design, but it received so violent a shock by the death of Elizabeth, as almost made us abandon all our hopes. Henry had no expectation that the powers of the North nor king James, the successor to Elizabeth, when he was acquainted with his character, would any of them so readily consent to support him in his design, as this princess had done. However, the new allies whom he daily gained in Germany (*g*), and even in Italy, comforted him a little for the loss of Elizabeth. The truce (*h*) between Spain and the Low Countries may also be numbered among the incidents favourable to it.

Yet, if we consider all the obstacles which afterwards arose in his own kingdom, from the protestants, the catholics, the clergy, nay, even from his own council, it will appear as if all things conspired against it. Could it be imagined that Henry, in his whole council, should not find one person besides myself to whom he could, without danger, disclose the whole of his designs? or that the respect due to him could scarcely restrain those apparently most devoted to his service from treating as wild and extravagant chimeras whatever of the plan he had, with greatest circumspection, revealed to them? But nothing discouraged Henry, who was an able politician and a better judge than all his council and kingdom. When he perceived that, notwithstanding all these obstacles, affairs began, both at home and abroad, to appear in a favourable situation, he then considered the success as infallible.

Nor will this his judgment, when thoroughly considered, be found so presumptuous as from a slight examination it may to some appear. For what did he hereby require of Europe?

(*f*) Philip II. of Spain died in 1598.
(*g*) Notably Maurice of Hesse, the Elector Palatine, the Duke of Wurtemburg, and the Elector of Brandenburg.
(*h*) In 1609.

Nothing more than that Europe should promote the means whereby he proposed to stabilise Christendom in that position towards which it had, by his efforts, been tending for some time. These means he rendered so easy of execution that for their fulfilment there would be required scarcely as much as the princes of Europe would voluntarily sacrifice for advantages less real, certain or durable. What they would gain by it, besides the inestimable benefits arising from peace, would greatly exceed all the expenses they would incur. What reason then could any of them have to oppose it? and, if they did not oppose it, how could the house of Austria support itself against powers who would have risen as open and secret enemies in the hope of depriving it of that strength which it had used only to oppress them? In other words, the house of Austria would have to face a united and hostile Europe. Nor would these princes have any reason to be jealous of the restorer of their liberty, for he was so far from seeking to re-imburse himself for all the expenses which his generosity would hereby involve, that his intention was voluntarily and for ever to relinquish all power of augmenting his dominions, not only by conquest, but by all other just and lawful means.

By this he would have convinced all his neighbours that his whole design was to save, both himself and them, those immense sums which the maintenance of so many thousand soldiers, so many fortified places, and so many military expenses requires; to free them for ever from the fear of those bloody catastrophes so common in Europe; to procure them an uninterrupted repose; and, finally, to unite them all in an indissoluble bond of security and friendship, after which they might live together like brethren, and reciprocally visit like good neighbours without the trouble of ceremony and without the expense of a train of attendants which princes use at best only for ostentation and frequently to conceal their misery. Does it not indeed reflect shame and reproach on a people who affect to be so polished and refined in their manners that all their pretended improvements have not yet guarded them from these barbarities which they detest in nations the most savage and uncultivated? To destroy these pernicious seeds of confusion and disorder, and prevent the barbarities of which they are the cause, could any scheme have been more happily and perfectly contrived than that of Henry the Great?

Here then is all that could be reasonably expected or required. It is only in the power of man to prepare and act, success is the work of a more mighty hand. Sensible people cannot be blamed for being prejudiced in favour of the scheme in question, from this circumstance only, that it was formed by the two potentates whom posterity will always consider as the most perfect models of the art of governing. In regard to Henry in particular I insist that it belongs only to princes who, like him, have had a constant succession of obstacles to encounter in all their designs. These are the princes who alone are privileged to judge what are real obstacles; and when we behold them willing to lay down their lives in support of their opinions, surely we may abide by their sentiments, without fear of being deceived. For my own part, I shall always think with regret that France, by the blow which it received from the loss of this great prince, was deprived of a glory far superior to that which his reign had acquired. There remains only to explain the several parts of the design, and the manner in which they were to be executed. We will begin by what relates to religion.

Two religions principally prevail in Christendom, the Roman and the Reformed; but, as this latter admits of several variations in its worship, which render it, if not as uniform as the roman, at least as far from being re-united, it is therefore necessary to divide it in two, one of which may be called the reformed, and the other the protestant religion (i). The manner in which these three religions prevail in Europe is extremely various. Italy and Spain remain in possession of the roman religion, pure and without mixture of any other. The reformed religion subsists in France with the roman, only under favour of the edicts, and is the weakest. England, Denmark, Sweden, the Low Countries, and Switzerland, have also a mixture of the same kind, but with this difference, that in them the protestant is the governing religion, the others are only tolerated. Germany unites all these and in several of its circles, as well as in Poland, shews them equal favour. I say nothing of Muscovy and Russia. These vast

(i) That is, the Calvinist and the Lutheran.

countries, which are not less than six hundred leagues in length and four hundred in breadth, being in great part still idolaters, and in part schismatics, such as Greeks and Armenians, have introduced so many superstitious practices in their worship, that there scarce remains any conformity with us among them; besides, they belong to Asia at least as much as to Europe. We may indeed almost consider them as a barbarous country, and place them in the same class with Turkey, though for these five hundred years, we have ranked them among the christian powers.

Each of these three religions being now established in Europe in such a manner that there is not the least appearance that any of them can be destroyed and experience having sufficiently demonstrated the inutility and danger of such an enterprise, the best therefore that can be done, is to preserve, and even strengthen all of them in such a manner that indulgence may not become an encouragement to the production of new sects or opinions which should carefully be suppressed on their first appearance. God Himself, by manifestly supporting what the catholics were pleased to call the new religion, has taught us this conduct which is not less conformable to the Holy Scripture than confirmed by its examples; and besides, the unsurmountable difficulty of forcing the pope's authority where it is no longer acknowledged renders what is here proposed absolutely necessary. Several cardinals equally sagacious and zealous and even some popes as Clement VIII. and Paul V. were of this opinion (k).

All therefore that remains now to be done is to strengthen the nations who have made choice of one of these religions in the principles they profess, as there is nothing in all respects so pernicious as a liberty in belief; and those nations, whose inhabitants profess several or all these religions should be careful to observe those rules necessary to remedy the ordinary inconveniences of a toleration in other respects beneficial. Italy, therefore, professing the roman religion and being moreover the residence of the popes, should preserve this religion in all its purity, and there would be no hardship in obliging all its

(k) Though it was Clement VIII. who absolved Henry, neither he nor his successor, Paul V. can be credited with very advanced views on toleration.

inhabitants either to conform to it or quit the country. The same regulations, very nearly, might be observed in regard to Spain. In such states as that of France where there is at least a governing religion, whoever should think the regulation too severe, by which calvinism would be always subordinate to the religion of their prince, might be permitted to depart the country. No new regulations would be necessary in any of the other nations, no violence on this account, but liberty unrestrained, seeing this liberty is become even a fundamental principle in their governments (*l*).

Thus we may perceive every thing on this head might be reduced to a few maxims, so much the more certain and invariable, as they were not contrary to the sentiments of any one. The protestants are very far from pretending to force their religion upon any of their neighbours by whom it is not voluntarily embraced. The catholics doubtless are of the same sentiments, and the pope would receive no injury in being deprived of what he confesses himself not to have possessed for a long time. His sacrificing these chimerical rights would be abundantly compensated by the regal dignity with which it would be proper to invest him and by the honour of being afterwards the common mediator between all the christian princes, a dignity which he would then enjoy without jealousy and for which it must be confessed the papal office has shown itself, by sagacious conduct, most peculiarly fitted.

Another point of the political scheme which also concerns religion, relates to the infidel princes of Europe, and consists in forcing out of it those who refuse to conform to any of the christian doctrines of religion. Should the grand duke of Muscovy or czar of Russia, who is believed to be the ancient khan of Scythia, refuse to enter into the association after it is proposed to him, he ought to be treated like the Sultan of Turkey, deprived of his possessions in Europe, and confined to Asia only, where he might, as long as he pleased, and without any interruption from us, continue the wars in which he is almost constantly engaged against the Turks and Persians.

(*l*) That is, so long as their rulers neither change their religion nor are succeeded by rulers of a different religion. Sully's view on toleration is simply the orthodox " cujus regio, eius religio."

To succeed in the execution of this plan will not appear difficult
if we suppose that all the christian princes unanimously concurred
in it. It would only be necessary for each of them to contribute,
in proportion to their several abilities, towards the support of the
forces and all the other incidental expenses which the success of
such an enterprise might require. These respective quotas were
to have been determined by a general council of which we shall
speak hereafter.   The following is what Henry the Great had
himself conceived on this head.   The pope for this expedition
should have furnished eight thousand foot, twelve hundred horse,
ten cannons, and ten galleys; the emperor and the circles of
Germany, sixty thousand foot, twenty thousand horse, five large
cannons, and ten galleys or other vessels; the king of France,
twenty thousand foot, four thousand horse, twenty cannons, and
ten ships or galleys; Spain, Britain, Denmark, Sweden, and
Poland, the like number with France, observing only, that these
powers should together supply what belonged to the sea-service in
the manner most suitable to their respective conveniences and
abilities therein; the king of Bohemia, five thousand foot, fifteen
hundred horse, and five cannons; the king of Hungary, twelve
thousand foot, five thousand horse, twenty cannons, and six
ships; the duke of Savoy, or king of Lombardy, eight thousand
foot, fifteen hundred horse, eight cannons, and six galleys; the
republic of Venice, ten thousand foot, twelve hundred horse, ten
cannons, and twenty-five galleys; the republic of the Swiss
cantons, fifteen thousand foot, five thousand horse, and twelve
cannons; the republic of Holland, twelve thousand foot, twelve
hundred horse, twelve cannons, and twelve ships; the Italian
republics, ten thousand foot, twelve hundred horse, ten cannons,
and eight galleys; the whole together amounting to about two
hundred and seventy thousand foot, fifty thousand horse, two
hundred cannons, and one hundred and twenty ships or galleys,
equipped and maintained at the expense of those powers, each
contributing according to his particular proportion.

This armament of the princes and states of Europe appears so
inconsiderable and so little burdensome, when compared with the
forces which they usually keep on foot to awe their neighbours,
or perhaps their own subjects, that were it to have subsisted,

even perpetually, it would not have occasioned any inconvenience and would have been an excellent military academy. But since the enterprises for which it was destined, would not always have continued, the number and expense might have been diminished in proportion to the necessities which would have remained a constant factor. Moreover I am convinced that such an armament would have been so highly approved of by all these princes that after they had, with its help, conquered all those territories in Europe (which they would not willingly share with a stranger), they would seek to unite with these conquests such parts of Asia as are most commodiously situated and particularly the whole coast of Africa which is too near to our territories for our complete security. The only precaution to be observed in regard to these additional countries would have been to form them into new kingdoms, declare them united with the rest of the christian powers, and bestow them on different princes, carefully observing to exclude those who before bore rank among the sovereigns of Europe.

That part of the design which may be considered as purely political turned almost entirely on a first preliminary which, I think, would not have met with more difficulty than the preceding article. This was to divest the house of Austria of the empire and of all the possessions in Germany, Italy, and the Low Countries; in a word, to reduce it to the sole kingdom of Spain, bounded by the ocean, the Mediterranean, and the Pyrenean mountains. But that it might, nevertheless, be equally powerful with the other sovereignties of Europe, it should have Sardinia, Majorca, Minorca; and, in the other islands on its own coasts, the Canaries, the Azores, and Cape-Verde, with its possessions in Africa, Mexico and the American islands belonging to it: countries, which alone might suffice to found great kingdoms, finally, the Philippines, Goa, the Moluccas, and its other possessions in Asia.

From hence a method seems to present itself whereby the house of Austria might be made amends for what it would be deprived of in Europe, which is to increase its dominions in the three other parts of the world by assisting it to obtain and by declaring it the sole proprietor both of what we do know and what we may hereafter discover in those parts. We may suppose that on this occasion it would not have been necessary to use force to bring this house to concur in such a design and, indeed, even on this supposition it was not the prince of this house reigning in Spain, to whom these parts of the world were to be subjected, but to different princes, of the same or of different branches, who in acknowledgment of their possessions should only have rendered homage to the crown of Spain or, at most, a tribute as due to the original conquerors. This house, which is so very desirous of being the most powerful in the world, might hereby have continued to flatter itself with so pleasing a pre-eminence without the other powers being endangered by its pretended grandeur.

The steps taken by the house of Austria to arrive at universal monarchy which evidently appear from the whole conduct of Charles V. and his son have rendered this severity as just as it is necessary and I will venture to say that this house would not have had any reasonable cause to complain of it. It is true it would be deprived of the empire; but impartially considered it will appear that all the other princes of Germany and even of Europe have an equal right to it. Were it necessary to prove this we need only recollect on what conditions Charles V. himself, the most powerful of them all, was acknowledged emperor; conditions, which, at Smalcalde, he solemnly swore to observe, in presence of seven princes or electors and the deputies of twenty-four protestant towns, the landgrave of Hesse and the prince of Anhalt being speakers for them all. He swore never to act contrary to the established laws of the empire, particularly the famous Golden Bull, obtained under Charles IV., unless it were to amplify them and even that only with the express consent and advice of the sovereign princes of Germany; not to infringe nor deprive them of any of their privileges; not to introduce foreigners into their council; not to make either war or peace without their consent; not to bestow honours and employments but on natives of Germany; not to use any other but the German language in all writings; not to levy any taxes by his own authority, nor apply any conquests which might be made, to his own particular profit. He, in particular, formally renounced all pretences of hereditary right in his house to the imperial dignity and according to the several articles of the golden bull he swore never in his life-time to recognize a king of the Romans. When the protestants of Germany, after they had in a manner driven Ferdinand out of it, consented to have the imperial crown placed on his head, they were careful to make him renew his engagements in regard to all these articles and to all these new regulations relative to the free exercise of their religion.

As to the possessions of the house of Austria in Germany, Italy, and the Low Countries, acquired by tyrannical usurpation, it would, after all, be only depriving it of territories which it keeps at so prodigious an expense (I speak, in particular, of Italy and the Low Countries) as all its treasures of the Indies have not been able to defray: and besides, by investing it with the exclusive privilege above-mentioned, of gaining new establishments and appropriating to its own use the mines and treasures of the three other parts of the world, it would be abundantly indemnified; for these new acquisitions would be at least as considerable, and undoubtedly far more rich, than those already held. But what is here proposed must not be understood as if the other nations of Europe were excluded from all commerce with those countries; on the contrary, it should be free and open to every one and the house of Austria, instead of considering this stipulation, which is of the greatest consequence, as an infringement of its privileges, would rather have reason to regard it as a farther advantage.

From a farther examination and consideration of these dispositions I do not doubt but the house of Austria would have accepted the proposed conditions without being forced to it; but, supposing the contrary, what would a resistance have signified? The promise made to all the princes of Europe of enriching themselves by the territories of which this house was to be divested, would deprive it of all hopes of assistance from any of them.

Upon the whole then it appears that all parties would have been gainers by it and this was what assured Henry the Great of the success of his design. The empire would again become a dignity to which all princes, but particularly those of Germany, might aspire. This dignity would become so much the more desirable that, although in accordance with its original institution

no revenues would be annexed to it, the emperor would be
declared the first and chief magistrate of the whole christian
republic. And as we may suppose this honour would afterwards
be conferred only on the most worthy, all his privileges in this
respect, instead of being diminished, would be enlarged; his
authority over the Belgic and Helvetic republics would be more
considerable and upon every new election they would be obliged
to render him a respectful homage. The electors would still continue to enjoy the right of electing the emperor as well as of
maintaining the king of the Romans; with this restriction only,
that the election should not be made twice together out of the
same family. The first to have been elected in this manner was
the elector of Bavaria (m), who was also, in consequence of the
partition, to have had those territories possessed by the house of
Austria which joined to his own on the side of Italy.

The rest of these territories were to have been divided and
equally distributed by the kings of France, England, Denmark,
and Sweden among the Venetians (n), the Grisons (o), the duke
of Wurtemburg, and the marquis of Baden, Anspach, and Dour-
lach (p). Bohemia was to have been constituted an elective
kingdom by annexing to it Moravia, Silesia, and Lusatia.
Hungary was also to have been an elective kingdom and the pope,
the emperor, the kings of France, England, Denmark, Sweden,
and Lombardy were to have had the right of nomination to it
and because this kingdom may be considered as the barrier of
Christendom against the infidels, it was to have been rendered
the most powerful and able to resist them. This was to have
been done by adding to it the monarchy of Austria, Styria,
Carinthia, and Carniola and by afterwards incorporating with it

(m) Of the German princes, the Elector of Bavaria was the most consistent
ally of France at the time when Sully was compiling his Memoirs. On several
occasions he was the French nominee for the imperial dignity.

(n) Traditionally at enmity with her Spanish and Italian neighbours, the
policy of Venice constantly gravitated to alliance with France. Moreover, she
was the one " liberal " State in an ultramontane world.

(o) The Grisons were Protestants, and were of paramount importance in
Richelieu's foreign policy because they controlled one of the Alpine passes into
Italy.

(p) These German princes were members of the Evangelical Union formed in
1608 to secure the religious integrity of their respective States, to vote in the
Diet as one body, to settle their own disputes by arbitration, and to maintain
an army for defence. Henry IV. was godfather of this league.

whatever might be acquired in Transylvania, Bosnia, Sclavonia, and Croatia. The same electors were to have obliged themselves, by oath, to assist it upon all occasions and they were to have been particularly careful never to grant their suffrages from partiality, artifice, or intrigue but always to confer the dignity on a prince who, by his great qualifications, particularly for war, should be generally acknowledged as most proper. Poland being, from its nearness to Turkey, Muscovy, and Tartary in the same situation with Hungary was also to have been made an elective kingdom by the same eight potentates; and its power was to have been augmented by annexing to it whatever should be conquered from the infidels adjoining its own frontiers and by determining in its favour those disputes which it had with all its other neighbours. Switzerland, when augmented by Franche-comté, Alsace, Tyrol, and other territories was to have been united into a sovereign republic governed by a council or senate, of which the emperor, the princes of Germany, and the Venetians were to have been umpires.

The changes to be made in Italy were that the pope should be declared a secular prince bearing rank among the monarchs of Europe and under this title should possess Naples, Apulia, Calabria and all their dependencies, which should be indissolubly united to St. Peter's patrimony. But in case the holy father had opposed this, which indeed could scarce have been supposed, the disposition must then have been changed and the kingdom of Naples would have been divided and disposed as the electoral kings should have determined. Sicily was to have been ceded to the republic of Venice, by letters from the same eight principal potentates, upon condition that it should render homage for it to every pope, who should bear the title of Immediate Chief of the Whole Italian republic; otherwise (for this reason) called The republic of the Church. The other members of this republic were to have been Genoa, Florence, Mantua, Modena, Parma and Lucca, without any alterations in their government. Bologna and Ferrara were to have been rendered free cities and all these governments were every twenty years to have rendered homage to the pope their chief, by the gift of a crucifix of the value of ten thousand crowns.

Of the three great republics of Europe, it appears, upon the first glance, that this would have been the most brilliant and the richest. Nevertheless, it would not have been so; for what belonged to the duke of Savoy was not comprised herein. His territories were to have been constituted one of the greatest monarchies of Europe, hereditary to males and females, and to have borne the title of the kingdom of Lombardy; wherein, beside the territory so called, the Milanese and Montserrat would also have been comprised. The duke of Mantua, in exchange for these, was to have the duchy of Cremona. An authentic testimony of the institution would have been given by the pope, the emperor and the other sovereigns of the christian republic.

Among all these different dismemberings, we may observe that France reserved nothing for itself but the glory of distributing them with equity. Henry had declared this to be his intention long before. He even sometimes said, with equal moderation and good sense, that were these dispositions once firmly established, he would have voluntarily consented to have the extent of France determined by a majority of suffrages. Nevertheless, as the districts of Artois, Hainault, Cambresis, Tournay, Namur and Luxembourg might more suitably be annexed to France than to any other nation, they were to have been ceded to Henry but divided into ten distinct governments and bestowed on so many French princes or lords, all of them bearing rank as sovereigns (q).

In regard to England it was precisely the same: this was a determined point between Elizabeth and Henry, the two princes who were authors of the scheme. This was probably due to an observation made by this queen, that the Britannic isles, in all the different states through which they had passed, whether under one or several monarchs, elective, hereditary, masculine or feminine, and among all the variations of their laws and policy, had never experienced any great disappointments or misfortunes, but when their sovereigns had meddled in affairs out of their little continent. It seems, indeed, as if they were concentered in it even by nature, and their happiness appears to depend entirely on themselves and their having no concerns with their neighbours,

(q) Compare this with statements in second paragraph of p. 46. Sully might have removed this inconsistency if he himself had ever reduced the scheme to a composite whole.

provided that they seek only to maintain peace in the three nations subject to them, by governing each according to its own laws and customs. To render every thing equal between France and England, Brabant from the dutchy of Limbourg, the jurisdiction of Malines, and the other dependencies on Flemish Flanders, Gallican or Imperial, were to have been formed into eight sovereign fiefs, to be given to so many princes or lords of this nation.

These two parts excepted, all the rest of the seventeen United Provinces, whether belonging to Spain or not, were to be erected into a free and independent state under the title of the Belgic republic; though there was one other fief to be formed from them, bearing the title of a principality, to be granted to the prince of Orange; also some other inconsiderable indemnities for three or four other persons. The succession of Cleves was to have been divided among those princes whom the emperor would have deprived of it, as well as among some other princes of the same district, to whom the imperial towns situated therein would have been granted. Even Sweden and Denmark, though they were to be considered as under the influence of the same law which England and France had imposed on themselves, would, by this distribution, have enlarged their territories and acquired other considerable advantages. An end would have been put to the perpetual trouble which agitated these two kingdoms and this, I think, would have been rendering them no inconsiderable service. All these cessions, exchanges, and transpositions towards the north of Germany were to have been determined by the kings of France, England, Lombardy, and the republic of Venice.

And now perhaps the purport of the design may be perceived, which was to divide Europe equally among a certain number of powers and in such a manner that none of them might have cause either of envy or fear from the possessions or power of the others. The number of them was reduced to fifteen and they were of three kinds: six great hereditary monarchies, five elective monarchies, and four sovereign republics. The six hereditary monarchies were France, Spain, England or Britain, Denmark, Sweden, and Lombardy; the five elective monarchies were the Empire, the Papacy or Pontificate, Poland, Hungary, and

Bohemia; the four republics were the Venetian, the Italian, or what, from its dukes, may be called the ducal, the Swiss, Helvetic or Confederate, and the Belgic or Provincial republic.

The laws and ordinances proper tô cement a union between all these princes and to maintain that harmony which should be once established among them, the reciprocal oaths and engagements in regard both to religion and policy, the mutual assurances in respect of the freedom of commerce and the measures to be taken to make all these partitions with equity and to the general content and satisfaction of the parties: all these matters are to be understood; nor is it necessary to say any thing of the precaution taken by Henry in regard to them. The most that could have happened would have been some trifling difficulties which would easily have been obviated in the general council, representing all the states of Europe the establishment of which was certainly the happiest invention that could have been conceived for preventing those innovations often introduced by time into the wisest and most useful institutions.

The model of this general council of Europe had been formed on that of the ancient Amphictyons of Greece, with such alterations only as rendered it suitable to our customs, climate, and policy. It consisted of a certain number of commissaries, ministers, or plenipotentiaries from all the governments of the christian republic, who were to be constantly assembled as a senate, to deliberate on any affairs which might occur; to discuss the different interests, pacify the quarrels, clear up and determine all the civil, political, and religious affairs of Europe, whether within itself or with its neighbours. The form and manner of proceeding in the senate would have been more particularly determined by the suffrages of the senate itself. Henry was of opinion that it should be composed of four commissaries from each of the following potentates: The Emperor, the Pope, the kings of France, Spain, England, Denmark, Sweden, Lombardy, Poland, and the republic of Venice; and of two only from the other republics and inferior powers, which all together would have composed a senate of about sixty-six persons, who should have been re-chosen every three years.

In regard to the place of meeting, it remained to have been

determined whether it would be better for the council to be fixed
or ambulatory, divided in three, or united into one.   If it were
divided into three, each containing twenty-two magistrates, then
each of them must have been fixed in such a centre as should
appear to be most commodious, as Paris or Bourges for one, and
somewhere about Trente and Cracovia for the two others.   If it
were judged more expedient not to divide their assembly, whether
fixed or ambulatory, it must have been nearly in the centre of
Europe and would consequently have been fixed in some one of
the fourteen cities following: Metz, Luxembourg, Nancy,
Cologne, Mayence, Treves, Francfort, Wurtzbourg, Heidelberg,
Spire, Strasbourg, Bale, Bezancon.

Besides this general council, it would perhaps have been
proper to have constituted some others, of an inferior degree, for
the particular convenience of different districts.   For example,
were six such created, they might have been placed at Dantzig,
Nuremberg, Vienna, Bologna, Constance and the last, wherever
it should be judged most convenient for the kingdoms of France,
Spain, England and the Belgic republic.   But whatever the
number or form of these particular councils might have been, it
would have been absolutely necessary that they should be subordinate, and recur, by appeal, to the great general council, whose
decisions, when considered as proceeding from the united authority
of all the sovereigns, pronounced in a manner equally free and
absolute, must have been regarded as so many final and
irrevocable decrees.

But let us quit these speculative designs, in which practice
and experience would perhaps have caused many alterations; and
let us come to the means actually employed by Henry to facilitate
the execution of his great design.

To gain one of the most powerful princes of Europe, with whom
to concert all his designs, was what Henry had always considered
as of the utmost consequence: and this was the reason, that after
the death of Elizabeth, who had indissolubly united the interest
of the two crowns of France and England, every means was used
which might inspire her successor, king James, with all her
sentiments.   Had I but succeeded in the solemn embassy, the
particulars of which I have related already, so far as to have

gained this prince's consent to have his name appear openly with Henry's, this military confederacy, especially if it had, in like manner, been strengthened with the names of the kings of Denmark and Sweden, would have prevented the troubles and difficulties of many negotiations: but nothing farther could be obtained of the king of England than the same promises which were required of the other courts; namely, that he would not only not oppose the confederacy, but, when Henry had made his designs public, would declare himself in his favour, and contribute towards it in the same manner as the other powers interested therein. A means was indeed afterwards found to obtain the execution of this promise, in a manner so much the more easy as it did not disturb the natural indolence of this prince. This was, by getting what he hesitated to undertake in his own name, executed by his son, the prince of Wales, who, as soon as he had obtained his father's promise (that he would at least not obstruct his proceedings), anticipated Henry's utmost wishes, being animated with a thirst of glory, and desire to render himself worthy of the esteem and alliance of Henry, for he was to marry the eldest of the daughters of France. He wrote me several letters upon this subject and expressed himself in the manner I have mentioned. He also said that the king of France might depend on having six thousand foot and fifteen hundred horse, which he would undertake to bring into his service whenever they should be required: and this number was afterwards augmented by two thousand more foot, and eight cannons, maintained in all respects at the expense of England for three years at least. The king of Sweden did not shew himself less zealous for the common cause; and the king of Denmark also appeared to be equally well disposed in its favour.

In the mean time we were indefatigable in our negotiations in the different courts of Europe, particularly in the circles of Germany and the United Provinces, where the king, for this purpose, had sent Boisisse, Fresne-Canaye, Baugy, Ancel, and Bongars. The council of the States were very soon unanimous in their determinations: the prince of Orange sent the sieurs Malderet and Brederode from them to offer the king fifteen thousand foot and three thousand horse. They were soon followed

by the landgrave of Hesse, and the prince of Anhalt, to whom as
well as to the prince of Orange, the confederacy was obliged for
being increased by the duke of Savoy; by all of the reformed
religion in Hungary, Bohemia, and lower Austria; by many
protestant princes and towns in Germany; and by all the Swiss
Cantons of this religion. And when the succession of Cleves,
which the Emperor shewed himself disposed to usurp, became
another incentive to the confederacy, there was then scarce any
part of Germany that was not for us; which evidently appeared
from the result of the general assembly at Hall (r). The elector
of Saxony, who perhaps remained alone of the opposite party,
might have been embarrassed in an affair out of which he would
probably have found it difficult to extricate himself; and this was
to have been done by recalling to his memory the fate of the
branch of John Frederic, deprived of this electorate by
Charles V. (s).

There were several of these powers, in regard to whom I am
persuaded nothing would have been risked, by disclosing to them
the whole intent and scope of the design. On the contrary, they
would probably have seconded it with the greater ardour when
they found the destruction of Austrian grandeur was a determined
point. These powers were more particularly the Venetians, the
United Provinces, almost all the protestants, and especially the
evangelics of Germany. But as too many precautions could not
be taken to prevent the catholic powers from being prejudiced
against the new alliance in which they were to be engaged, a too
hasty discovery, either of the true motives, or the whole intent
of the design, was therefore cautiously avoided. It was at first
concealed from all without exception and afterwards revealed but
to a few persons of approved discretion and those only such as
were absolutely necessary to engage others to join the confederacy.
The association was for a long time spoken of to others only as a
kind of general treaty of peace, wherein such methods would be

(r) By the Treaty of Hall (1610), Henry IV. and the Evangelical Union
agreed to support the Elector of Brandenburg and Count Philip of Neuburg in
their claims to the Cleves-Julich territories.
(s) Presumably a threat. After the victory of Charles V. over the Protestants at Muhlberg (1547), the electorate of Saxony was transferred from the
elder (Ernestine) to the younger (Albertine) branch of the family. There
would therefore be good precedent for depriving the Elector should he refuse
to conform.

projected as the public benefit and the general service of Europe
might suggest as necessary to stop the progress of the excessive
power of the house of Austria. Our ambassadors and agents had
orders only to demand of these princes a renewal or commence-
ment of alliance, in order more effectually to succeed in the projected peace; to consult with them upon the means whereby to
effect it; to appear as if sent only for the purpose of joint enquiry
into the discovery of these means. According to the disposition
in which they found these princes, they were to insinuate, as if
by accidental conjecture, some notion of a new method for maintaining the equilibrium of Europe and for securing to each religion
a more undisturbed peace than it had hitherto enjoyed. The
proposals made to the kings of England and Sweden, and the
dukes of Savoy and Lorraine, for alliances by marriage, proved
very successful: it was absolutely determined that the dauphin
should espouse the heiress of Lorraine, which dutchy still continued, as before, to depend on the Empire.

But no precaution appeared so necessary, nor was more
strongly recommended to our negotiators, than to convince all
the princes of Europe of the disinterestedness with which Henry
was resolved to act on this occasion. This point was indefatigably
laboured, and they were convinced of it, when, on the supposition
that it would be necessary to have recourse to arms, we strongly
affirmed that the forces, the treasures, and even the person of
Henry, might be depended on; and this in a manner so generous
on his side, that, instead of expecting to be rewarded, or even
indemnified for them, he was voluntarily inclined to give the most
positive assurances, not to reserve to himself a single town, nor
the smallest district. This moderation, of which at last no one
doubted, made a suitable impression, especially when it was
perceived to be so much the more generous, as there was sufficient
to excite and satisfy the desires of all. And in the interim,
before the solemn publication of this absolute renunciation, which
was to have been made in the manifestoes that were preparing,
Henry gave a proof of it, in the form of an absolute demonstration
to the pope (t).

No one being ignorant that as it was, at least, intended to

(t) Compare this with p. 40.

deprive Spain of those of its usurpations which were the most manifestly unjust (Navarre and Rousillon would infallibly revert to France), the king therefore voluntarily offered to exchange them for the two kingdoms of Naples and Sicily and at the same time to make a present of both to the Pope and the republic of Venice. This, certainly, was renouncing the most incontestible right he could have to any of the territories of which this Crown was to be deprived; and by submitting this affair, as he did, to the determination of the Pope and the Venetians, he the more obviously obliged them, as both the honour and profit which might arise therefrom would be in their favour. The Pope, therefore, on the first proposition made to him, even anticipated Henry's intentions. He immediately demanded whether, as affairs were then circumstanced, the several powers would approve his taking upon him the office of common mediator, to establish peace in Europe and convert the continual wars among its several princes into a perpetual war against the infidels. This was a part of the design he had been very careful to acquaint him with: and the pope sufficiently shewed that he was desirous nothing should be done without his participation and that he was still less disposed to refuse the advantage offered to him.

Paul V. when a favourable opportunity offered, explained himself more openly on this head. Ubaldini, his nuncio, told the king that his holiness, for the confederacy against the house of Austria, would, on various pretences, engage to raise ten thousand foot, fifteen hundred horse, and ten cannons; provided that his majesty would promise to defray the necessary expenses of their subsistence for three years; would give all possible security for the cession of Naples, and the other rights of homage, according to promise; and would sincerely consent to the other conditions, in regard to the treaty that he should think necessary to impose. These conditions, at least the principal of them, were, that only catholics should be elected emperors; that the Roman religion should be maintained in all its rights, and ecclesiastics in all their privileges and immunities; and that the protestants should not be permitted to establish themselves in places where they were not established before the treaty. The king promised Ubaldini that he would religiously observe all these conditions and farther, he relinquished to the pope the honour of being the arbitrator of all those regulations to be made in the establishment of the new republic.

The removing of these difficulties in regard to the pope was of no inconsiderable consequence for his example would not fail to be of great force in determining the other catholic powers, especially those of Italy. Nothing was neglected which might promote the favourable dispositions in which they appeared to be, by punctually paying the cardinals and petty princes of Italy their pensions, and even by adding to them several other gratuities. The establishment of a new monarchy in Italy was the only pretence these petty courts had for not joining in the confederacy; but this vain apprehension would be easily dissipated. The particular advantages which each would acquire might alone have satisfied them in this respect; but if not, all opposers might have been threatened with being declared, after a certain time, divested of all right to the proposed advantages and even of all pretensions to the empire, or the elective kingdoms; and that the republics amongst them should be converted into sovereignties, and sovereignties into republics. There is but little probability that any of them would even have demurred what to do. The punishment of the first offender would have compelled the submission of all these petty states, who were besides sufficiently sensible of their impotence. But this method was not to be used but on failure of all others; and even then, no opportunity would have been neglected of shewing them favour.

And now we are arrived at the point to which every thing was advanced at the fatal moment of the death of Henry the Great; and the following is a circumstantial detail of the forces for the war (u), which all the parties concerned had, in conjunction with him, agreed to furnish. The contingents of the kings of England, Sweden, and Denmark were each eight thousand foot, fifteen hundred horse, and eight cannons, to be raised and maintained, in all respects, at their expense, at least for three years; and this expense, reckoning ten livres a month for each foot soldier, thirty livres for each trooper, the pay of the officers included, and the year to be composed of ten months, would amount, for each of

(u) Compare these figures with those already given on p. 34.

these states, to three millions three hundred and seventy thousand
livres for three years; the expense of the artillery, fifteen hundred
livres a month for each piece being also included. The princes
of Germany, before mentioned, were to furnish twenty-five
thousand foot, ten thousand horse, and forty cannons: they had
themselves computed the expense at nine or ten millions for three
years. The United Provinces, twelve thousand foot, two
thousand horse, and ten cannons: the expense twelve millions.
Hungary, Bohemia, and the other evangelics of Germany, the
same number, and nearly at the same expense. The Pope, ten
thousand foot, fifteen hundred horse, and eight cannons. The
duke of Savoy, eighteen thousand foot, two thousand horse, and
twelve cannons. The Venetians, twelve thousand foot, two
thousand horse, and twelve cannons. The expense of these last
mentioned armaments the king himself had engaged to defray.
The total of all these foreign forces, allowing for deficiencies,
which might probably have happened, would always have been,
at least one hundred thousand foot, from twenty to twenty-five
thousand horse and about one hundred and twenty cannons.

The king, on his side, had actually on foot two good and well
furnished armies; the first, which he was to have commanded in
person, consisted of twenty thousand foot, all native French,
eight thousand Switzers, four thousand Lansquenets or Walloons,
five thousand horse, and twenty cannons. The second, to be
commanded by Lesdiguières, in the neighbourhood of the Alps,
consisted of ten thousand foot, one thousand horse, and ten
cannons; besides a flying camp, of four thousand foot, six hundred
horse, and ten cannons; and a reserve of two thousand foot to
garrison such places where they might be necessary. We will
make a general calculation of all these troops.

The twenty thousand foot, at twenty-one livres a month to each
man, including the appointments of generals and officers, would,
by the month, require four hundred and twenty thousand livres,
and by the year, five millions and forty thousand livres; the eight
thousand Switzers and four thousand Lasquenets, three millions;
the five thousand horse, at sixty livres a month to each, by the
month, would require two hundred and forty thousand livres, and
by the year, two millions eight hundred and forty thousand livres.

This computation is made so high as sixty livres a month to each, because the pay of the officers, and particularly of the king's body-guard, composed of a thousand men of the first rank in the kingdom, who served as volunteers, was therein included. The expense of the twenty large cannons, six culverins, and four demi-culverins, supposing all necessary furniture for them provided, would amount to three thousand six hundred livres a month for each piece; the thirty together would consequently require one hundred and eight thousand livres. Extraordinary expenses and losses, in regard to the provisions and ammunition for his army, might be computed at one hundred and fifty thousand livres.

And for expenses, whether ordinary or extraordinary, in spies, for sick and wounded, and other unforeseen contingencies, computing at the highest, a like sum of one million eight hundred thousand livres. To supply the deficiencies which might happen in the armies of the confederate princes, to pay the pensions, and to answer other particular exigencies which might arise in the kingdom, three hundred thousand livres a month; for the year, three millions six hundred thousand livres. The army of Lesdiguières would require three millions a year; and as much for each of the armies of the Pope, the Venetians, and the duke of Savoy. These four last articles together, make twelve millions a year; which, added to the preceding sums amount in the whole to about thirty millions one hundred and sixty thousand livres a year.

It remains only to triple this total for three years, during which it was supposed there might be occasion for the forces, and the whole amount will appear to be between ninety and ninety-one millions, which might perhaps be necessary to defray the expenses of the intended war. I say perhaps, for in this calculation I have not included the flying camp, nor the two thousand men for garrisons: the first of these two, at the rate of eighteen livres a month to each foot soldier, and fifty livres to each trooper, would require a farther sum of about one hundred and thirty thousand livres a month; which, for a year, would be one million five hundred thousand livres, and four millions five hundred thousand livres for three years: the second for the three years, would require about twelve hundred thousand livres.

On a supposition that the expense of France, on this occasion, would not have amounted to more than between ninety and ninety-five millions (which supposition is far from being hazardous, because we have here computed every thing at the highest it would bear), it is easy to shew that, at the expiration of three years, Henry would have remaining in his coffers thirty millions over and above what would be expended, the total amount of all the receipts from the several funds, formed and to be formed for these three years, being one hundred and twenty-one millions five hundred and forty thousand livres, as appears from the three estimates which I drew up and presented to his majesty.

The first of these estimates, which contained only a list of the sums actually deposited in the Bastile, amounted to twenty-two millions four hundred and sixty thousand livres, in several coffers, marked Phelipeaux, Puget, and Bouhier. The second was another list of the sums actually due from the farmers (r), partisans, and receivers-general which might be considered as in possession, and produced another total of eighteen millions six hundred and thirteen thousand livres. These two totals together made forty-one millions seventy-three thousand livres which the king would immediately have at his disposal. To acquire the rest of these hundred and twenty-one millions, I had no recourse, in the third estimate, to any new taxations. The whole remainder would arise solely from the offers of augmentation upon the several royal revenues which the farmers and partisans (w) had made for a lease of three years, and from what the officers of justice and the finances had voluntarily engaged to furnish, provided they might be permitted the free enjoyment of certain privileges: so that in these one hundred twenty-one millions, I had not comprehended the three years receipts of the other royal revenues. And in case it were afterwards necessary to have recourse to means somewhat more burthensome, I had given the king another estimate, whereby, instead of these one hundred and

(r) That is, the tax-farmers.
(w) The "partisans" were a hated class who, when ready money was short, would advance a portion ("parti") of the expected total yield of a tax and then recoup themselves by extracting the full amount of the tax from those on whom it was levied. Although Sully, as Superintendent of Finance, effected several reforms, he was never able to eradicate the vicious system by which, in the absence of a civil service, the taxes were battened upon by a host of human parasites.

twenty-one millions, it appeared that one hundred and seventy-five millions might have been raised. I also demonstrated, that, upon any pressing emergency, this kingdom could open itself resources of treasure that are almost innumerable.

It was very much to be wished that the sums of money and the number of men to be furnished by the other confederates would be equally well secured by such estimates. But whatever deficiencies might have happened, having forty-one millions to distribute wherever it might be found necessary, what obstacles could Henry have to fear from a power which was known to be destitute of money, and even of troops? no one being ignorant, that the best and most numerous forces which Spain had in its service were drawn from Sicily, Naples, and Lombardy or else were Germans, Switzers, and Walloons.

Every thing therefore concurring to promote success, and good magazines being placed in proper parts of the passage, the king was on the point of marching, at the head of his army, directly to Mezières; from whence, taking his route by Clinchamp, Orchimont, Beauraing, Offais, Longpré, &c. after having caused five forts to be erected in these quarters, and therein placed his two thousand men destined for that purpose, with the necessary provisions and ammunition, he would, near Duren and Stavelo, have joined the two armies, which the princes of Germany and the United Provinces would have caused to march thither. Thereupon beginning by occupying all those passages through which the enemy might find entrance into the territories of Juliers and Cleves, these principalities, which were a pretext for the armament, would consequently have immediately submitted to him and would have been sequestrated, till it should appear how the Emperor and the king of Spain would act in regard to the designs of the confederate princes.

This was the moment fixed on to publish and make known throughout Europe, the declarations, in form of manifestoes, which were to open the eyes of all in regard to their true interests and the real motives which had caused Henry and the confederate princes thus to take up arms. These manifestoes were composed with the greatest care; a spirit of justice, honesty, and good faith, of disinterestedness and good policy, were every where apparent

in them. Without wholly revealing the several changes intended
to be made in Europe, it was intimated that their common
interest had thus compelled its princes to arm themselves; not
only to prevent the house of Austria from getting possession of
Cleves, but also to divest her of the United Provinces, and of
whatever else she unjustly possessed; that their intentions were
to distribute these territories among such princes and states as
were the weakest; that the design was such, as could not surely
give occasion to a war in Europe; that, though armed, the kings of
France and the North rather chose to be mediators in the causes
of complaint which Europe, through them, made against the house
of Austria, and only fought amicably to determine all differences
subsisting among the several princes; and that whatever was
done on this occasion should be not only with the unanimous
consent of all these powers, but even of all their people, who
were hereby invited to give in their opinions to the confederate
princes. Such also would have been the substance of the circular
letters which Henry and the associated princes would at the same
time send to all places subject to them; that so the people
being informed, and joining their suffrages, a universal cry from
all parts of Christendom would have been raised against the house
of Austria.

As it was determined to avoid, with the utmost caution, whatever might give umbrage to any one, and Henry being desirous
to give still more convincing proofs to his confederates that to
promote their true interests was his sole study and design; to
these letters already mentioned he would have added others to
be written to different courts, particularly to the electors of
Cologne and Treves, the bishops of Munster, Liège, and Paderborn
and the duke and duchess of Lorraine. This conduct would have
been pursued in regard even to our enemies, in the letters which
were to be written to the archduke, and the infanta his wife, to
the Emperor himself, and to all the Austrian princes, requesting
them, from the strongest and most pressing motives, to embrace
the only right and reasonable party. In all places, nothing would
have been neglected, to instruct, convince, and gain confidence;
the execution of all engagements, and the distribution or seques-
tration of whatever territories might require to be so disposed

would have been strictly, and even scrupulously, observed; force would never have been employed, till arguments, entreaties, embassies, and negotiations should have failed; finally, even in the use of arms, it would have been not as enemies, but pacifiers. The queen would have advanced as far as Metz, accompanied by the whole court, and attended by such pomp and equipage as were suitable only to peace.

Henry had projected a new method of discipline in his camp, which very probably would have produced the good effects intended by it, especially if his example had been imitated by the other princes his allies. He intended to have created four marshals of France, or at least four camp marshals, whose sole care should have been to maintain universal order, discipline, and subordination. The first of these would have had the inspection of the cavalry, the second of the French infantry, the third of the foreign forces, and the fourth of whatever concerned the artillery, ammunition, and provisions and the king would have required an exact and regular account from these officers of whatever was transacted by them in their respective divisions. He applied himself with equal ardour to make all military virtues revered and honoured in his army by granting all employs and places of trust to merit only, by preferring good officers, by rewarding good soldiers, by punishing blasphemies and other impious language, by shewing a regard both for his own troops and those of his confederates, by stifling a spirit of discord, caused by a difference or religions and, finally, by uniting emulation with that harmony of sentiments which contributes more than all the rest to obtain victory.

The consequence of this enterprise, with regard to war, would have depended on the manner in which the Emperor and the king of Spain would receive the propositions and their reply to the manifestoes of the confederate princes. It seems probable that the emperor, submitting to force, would have consented to every thing. I am even persuaded he would have been the first to demand an amicable interview with the king of France, that he might at least extricate himself with honour out of the difficulties in which he would have been involved and he would probably have been satisfied with assurances that the imperial dignity, with all its rights and prerogatives, should be secured to him for his life. The archdukes had made great advances; they engaged to permit the king, with all his troops, to enter their territories and towns, provided they committed no hostilities in them and paid punctually, in all places, for whatever they required. If these appearances were not deceitful, Spain being abandoned by all, must, though unwillingly, have submitted to the will of its conquerors.

But it may be supposed, that all the branches of the house of Austria would, on this occasion, have united, and, in defence of their common interests, would have used all the efforts of which they were capable. In this case, Henry and the confederate princes would declare war in form against their enemies and deprived the Spaniards of all communications, especially with the Low Countries after having, as we have said, united all their forces, given audience to the princes of Germany, promised assistance to the people of Hungary and Bohemia who should come to implore it of them, and finally, secured the territory of Cleves. These princes would then have caused their three armies to advance towards Bale and Strasbourg to support the Switzers, who after having, for form's sake, asked leave of the emperor, would have declared for the union. The United Provinces, though at a considerable distance from these armies, would yet have been sufficiently defended by the flying camp, which Henry would have caused to advance towards them, by the arms of England and the North, to whose protection they would be entrusted, by the care which at first would have been taken to get possession of Charlemont, Maestricht, Namur, and other places near the Meuse, and finally, by the naval forces of these provinces, which, in conjunction with those of England, would have reigned absolute masters at sea.

These measures being taken, the war could have fallen only in Italy or Germany and supposing it to have happened in the former, the three armies of Henry, the prince of Orange, and the princes of Germany, quitting Franche-Comté, after having fortified it in the same manner as the Low Countries by a small body of troops, would have marched with their forces towards the Alps, where they would have been joined by those of Lesdiguières,

the pope, the Venetians, and the duke of Savoy. These latter
would then have declared themselves openly; the duke of Savoy,
by requiring a portion for his duchess, equal to what had been
given to the infanta Isabella and the other powers, by demanding
the execution of the agreement in regard to Navarre, Naples, and
Sicily. Thus, from all parts of Europe, war would be
declared against Spain. If the enemy should appear inclined to
draw the war into Germany, then the confederates, having left a
considerable number of troops in Italy, would have penetrated
even into the heart of Germany, where, from Hungary and
Bohemia, they would have been strengthened by those powerful
succours which were there preparing.

The other events, in consequence of these dispositions, can only
be conjectured, because they would greatly depend on the degree
of alacrity with which the enemy should oppose the rapidity of
our conquests and on the readiness with which the confederates,
especially those at the extremity of Germany, should make good
their engagements. Nevertheless, I am persuaded that, from the
dispositions as here laid down, there are none but must regard
the house of Austria as penetrated by the blow whose force was
for ever to annihilate its power and open a passage to the execution of the other projected designs, to which this attack could
only be considered as the preliminary. I will add too (and here
the voice of all Europe will vindicate me from the imputation of
partiality) that if the force necessary to render such an enterprise
successful does always depend on the person of the chief who
conducts it, this could not have been better conferred than upon
Henry the Great. With a valour alone capable of surmounting
the greatest difficulties and a presence of mind which neither
neglected nor lost any opportunities; with a prudence which,
without precipitating any thing, or attempting too many things
at a time, could regularly connect them together and perfectly
knew what might and what might not be the result of time; with
a consummate experience; and finally, with all those other great
qualifications, whether as a warrior or politician, which were so
remarkable in this prince; what is there which might not have
been obtained? This was the meaning of that modest device
which this great king caused to be inscribed on some of the last
medals that were struck under his reign, *Nil sine consilio.*

THE GROTIUS SOCIETY PUBLICATIONS.

Texts for Students of International Relations.

No. 3.

HUGONIS GROTII

DE JURE BELLI AC PACIS

LIBRI TRES.

SELECTIONS

TRANSLATED, WITH AN INTRODUCTION

BY

W. S. M. KNIGHT,

*Of New College, Oxford, and of the Inner Temple,
Barrister-at-Law.*

Price 2/6 net.

SWEET AND MAXWELL, LIMITED,

3 CHANCERY LANE, LONDON, W.C. 2.

1922.

PRINTED AT READING, ENGLAND
BY
THE EASTERN PRESS, LIMITED

CONTENTS.

INTRODUCTION.

Huig de Groot, better known as Hugo Grotius, ranks amongst the world's greatest men. He wrote several books of highest distinction, but it is upon his *De Jure Belli* that his permanent fame rests. To introduce the following selection from that work, we propose here very briefly to sketch his life and indicate, from a particular point of view, his place and importance in the succession of international jurists.

Grotius was born in the year 1583 at Delft, then the political capital of the revolting Dutch Netherlands His family had long occupied an influential position in the government of the city, and was also closely akin to many of the other Dutch ruling families of the period. His father, a wealthy and cultured man with important political associations, served his turn as burgomaster, and held the high office of Curator of the University of Leyden. His education, from its beginnings, was of the best offered in Holland, then the most vigorous child of the Renaissance. From his infancy, at home, he was nurtured in the humanities and science, in a circle in which the leading professors of the university —including Scaliger, Lipsius and Simon Stevin—were most honoured intimates. At the university itself, entering before he was twelve years of age and leaving at fifteen, Grotius, already in his earlier years having been the resident pupil of the most famous of Dutch divines, Uytenbogart, was the special protégé of Scaliger and dwelt beneath the roof of Francis Junius, the chief of the continental reformed clergy.

Upon leaving the university, Grotius was immediately introduced to the world of public affairs, and that under the wing of the great statesman, Barneveld. In his train the young Grotius journeyed on a diplomatic mission to France. Here he came into touch with Henry IV. and, later, remaining in the country after the departure of the diplomats, completed the study of the law at a

French university. At eighteen years of age he was back in his native land, established at The Hague, there, in association with Barneveld and the Dutch East India merchants, to settle down to the practice of the law. Within seven years he was successively Historiographer of Holland and Advocate-Fiscal, and, with a legal practice of the best class, a leader of the Dutch Bar. In 1613, just appointed Pensionary of Rotterdam, a high legal office which carried with it seats in the States of Holland and the Dutch States-General, he was included in a mission to England to oppose, on behalf of the Dutch East India Company, the principle of the freedom of the seas—the principle for which were fighting the English adventurers in the Far East (a). And during this visit to England, Grotius, as spokesman of a considerable party in his country, seized the opportunity personally to press King James to convene an international council to elaborate a scheme for reuniting the divided Churches of Christendom.

Back in Holland, after some intimate association with James I. and Casaubon, as also with Bishop Andrewes and other leaders of the English High Church party, Grotius threw himself into the Arminian controversy, in which, since its beginnings, he had taken a keen personal interest. Though apparently purely a theological contention, this, like most contemporary religious questions, was equally a struggle of political ideas. His side was that of the Arminians; his leader, Barneveld. Prince Maurice, the Stadtholder, stood for the other side, that of the Calvinists. Thus Grotius became a politician. And a politician, too, who— such was the course of events—was at the same time, in the judgment of his opponents, a conspirator against the peace and security of his country, and, as such, was eventually arrested and convicted and imprisoned for life. Barneveld was executed. But history, though completely justifying the policy of Maurice, does, almost with one voice, declare that Grotius was a true patriot and an injured man, unjustly and illegally condemned.

Imprisoned for life in the year 1619, at the age of thirty-six, the career of Grotius might be regarded as at an end. It was not

(a) There is a very general misconception both as to the date of the visit of Grotius to England and as to the object of the visit. It is somewhat of a shock to discover that the duty of the author of the *Mare Liberum*, which he most ably and quite readily performed, was to struggle for the principle of the *mare clausum* and counter the arguments of his own book.

so, however, for, managing to escape, he fled to France, arriving in Paris in April, 1621. There he remained, save for a short interval, for the rest of his life, an exile. And there, within the next few years, he wrote and published his great work, the *De Jure Belli*. But this was not a first book, the work of one who, hitherto exclusively a politician and man of affairs, had now, when fallen, turned to literature and philosophy in order to while away the tedium of banishment. As a fact, his natural bent had always been towards scholarship and literature, and it was not until he was well established in legal practice and deep in politics that he was able, apparently much against his inclinations, to resign himself primarily to the life of a man of affairs. And even then, far from losing touch with his old interests, he continued keenly to cultivate learning, never failing, also, to keep abreast with the progress of science.

As a child he had composed some warmly applauded Latin verse, and before he died he was acclaimed one of the three best Latin poets of his age. When only a boy, he had completed, with some assistance from Scaliger and his father, a critical edition of the *Satyricon* of Martianus Capella: at sixteen years of age he had translated into Latin, with an introduction of his own, Stevin's famous little handbook on navigation, *The Haven-Finder*; and at about the same time he brought out a new edition of the *Phenomena* of Aratus. Amongst other labours in the field of scholarship are editions of Theocritus, Lucan and Stobaeus. There are also two important original Latin tragedies. Of one of these, the *Adamus Exul* (sic), published in 1601, it has been charged against Milton that he deliberately plagiarised it in *Paradise Lost*. The other, *Christus Patiens*—its subject the Passion of our Lord—appeared in 1608, and secured for its author a wide and lasting reputation. In history he had published a work on the origins of the Dutch Republic, and, on politics, we have a number of works, all controversial, suggested by the politico-ecclesiastical difficulties of his day. Of greater importance, however, is a small work on the Dutch government, to be developed, later, in a posthumous treatise on sovereignty, *De imperio summarum potestatum circa sacra*, which, while deriving from postulates of political particularism the Dutch principles of religious toleration, immediately became a leading authority for the upholders of the *jus divinum*.

Theology, however, was his preoccupation. His poems, hitherto, had been very largely inspired by sacred subjects—his tragedies the tale of some Divine drama and his lesser and fugitive verse generally either comment on or paraphrase of Scripture. In prose, his distinction was as marked in this branch of literature as in any other he had touched, the most outstanding of his works of this period being his *Defensio fidei Catholicae*, which introduced an interesting modification of the traditional doctrine of the Atonement. In prison, even, Grotius had not been idle. He had written the first sketch of an introductory treatise on Dutch law— still a standard text-book—and also a slight work on Christian apologetics, which—defending, long before such a work was attempted in England, the Christian dogmas common to the various confessions—developed later on into the famous *Truth of the Christian Religion*, to be read and studied, until our own time, in almost every land and language.

But long before this he had written the *De Jure Praedae*, and published, in 1608, its twelfth chapter, the *Mare Liberum*—that great little legal classic in which he asserts the principle of the freedom of the seas, compelling reply from Welwood and Selden. This, Grotius had published anonymously; but that he was its author was quite well known five years afterwards, in 1613, when, in England, as practical man of affairs and advocate for the Dutch traders to the East, and against the English, he is to be found—as we have already noted—frankly and energetically repudiating and denying that principle with all the wealth of his dialectic and learning.

So we have Grotius—scholar, poet, literary man and jurist, as well as politician and theological partisan. Already distinguished, too, in all. And, like so many of the great figures of his period, he was essentially a man of action, and a very human man too. His political activities and his escape from prison alone are proof of his alertness and vitality and untiring energy. Though, on occasion, free and easy in his relations with the people, he was yet exclusive and aristocratic. He seems to have intensely loved personal display, association with the great, and sharing in the ruling of men and the intrigues of statecraft. He was a restless man, quick to defend, by arms or the duel, his cause or honour or even a mere point of etiquette—far, indeed, personally, from being a "pacifist," whether in public affairs or in private. Yet, withal, his nature was a profoundly spiritual one. And this though his rivals and opponents found him to be a "busy" man, too "pushing" and somewhat unscrupulous and self-assertive, one with whom they must deal most warily—not one to be entirely trusted. Such is the man we find in France, an exile. And having regard to what he had already accomplished, to the then political state of Europe, and to the bent of his genius, it is no matter for surprise that he determined to write a book, and that to be one on International Right. So it came about that, after working upon it during a period of just over two years, Grotius gave to the world, in the year 1625, his great masterpiece, the *De Jure Belli.*

The work commanded an instant and permanent reputation and success. Fifty-six editions can be counted. It became, for centuries, a leading text-book and was even made the subject of a special professorial chair.

At the foundation of the system of International Right—or, rather, perhaps, of ethics—which is so elaborately exposed by Grotius in this great work, lies the doctrine of Justice—very root and essence of that system. And this Justice, as he unfolds and applies it, has little or nothing in common with the justice so variously defined and developed in later and modern times. Grotius does not derive his doctrine from positive law. Nor, for him, has justice its yet deeper foundation in the conditions of human existence. On the contrary, the method of Grotius is deductive, save for some unconscious induction based upon material supplied by Roman law; and thus his doctrine of Justice is substantially identical with that which, for centuries before his day, had been gradually elaborated by the Catholic philosophers and divines, and at the Reformation taken over by the earlier Protestants. Its origins are to be found in Aristotle. But "the noble, beautiful, and altogether rational edifice" had been raised on the vestiges of Stoicism as found in Cicero, and on the writings of St. Augustine, most generally by scholastics, such as St. Thomas Aquinas—strongly influenced by the renascent Roman law—and, later, Soto, Molina and Suarez. In relation to fundamentals, the place of Grotius is thus in the line of the scholastic succession. Justice was for him the most important of the cardinal virtues—it might even be the sum of all the virtues.

It is a moral faculty or habit which perfects the will and inclines it to render to each and to all that which is their due.

Invested with God-given faculties—primordial, antecedent to and independent of society and State—man is under prime obligation to devote their exercise to a conduct of life in harmony with Divine intention. His right is the correlative of that obligation. His " natural rights "—that primordial right resolved by " the spectral analysis of the law of nature into its prismatic colours "—being derived through nature from their sacred source, are thus as inviolable as sacred. And these natural rights, together with all other man's rights, whether granted by Church or State or acquired by his own industry and ability, are the object of the virtue of Justice.

Then, following the scholastics, Grotius insists upon the Aristotelian distinction between Expletory and Attributive Justice. A right in the strict sense, or a claim in justice, is not a merely vague and indefinite claim against others which they are always bound to respect. It is a moral and lawful faculty of doing, possessing, or exacting something. But when such a right is asserted it is Expletory or legal Justice that is invoked, as in a court of law, in order that he who invokes it may receive his due, for Expletory Justice requires that all should have what belongs to them. What principle, then, is it that determines what does belong to a man? That of Attributive Justice, which is administered by a society at large, a State, through a legislature rather than by a court of law, in exercise of its power to realise its own end without violation of the natural rights of its members or subjects. Its principle is that all the members of the society should each enjoy his " deserts," that is to say, not his moral worth, but, so far as circumstances permit, his due share of the general weal, regard being had to his personal contribution thereto. And the claim which a man has to the exercise of this justice is termed an " aptitude," or, in modern English, a moral right, as distinguished from a faculty, or legal right, which comes into existence only after an exercise of Attributive Justice in order that such justice may be enforced.

But Justice, or rather *jus*, has another and yet wider signification. It means law in its most general sense, that is to say, a " rule of moral acts obliging to that which is right " or " upright "—

" right " here including the matter not only of Justice but also of the other cardinal virtues. Only loosely can such right be called just, however, for its correlative, in many instances, may be but the object of a virtue which has no inherent association with obligation. This *jus*, Justice or law, is either Natural or Positive.

Natural Law—and here we seem to be thrown back by Grotius upon his fundamental conception of Justice as a virtue—deals not only with things made by Nature herself, but also with things produced by the act of man, and is immutable—unchangeable even by God Himself. It is the law of God as disclosed by Nature to the reason of man. It is, in fact, *jus* properly and strictly so called, and is derived from two sources—the tendency to the conservation of society and the free will of God. By this law things are obligatory or forbidden by their very nature, and man can by no means change their inherent characteristic. That there is such a thing as Natural Law is proved, *a priori*, by showing the agreement or disagreement of anything with the rational and social nature of man, and *a posteriori*, when by certain or very probable accounts anything is found to be accepted as Natural Law among all nations, or at least among the more civilised.

Here, Grotius must be regarded as attempting to develop a Protestant ethic, as foundation for a theory of world-unity, following a path which had already been opened up by Ockham and others, among the scholastics, and pursued more recently by the later scholastics as well as by the humanists and earlier reformers. Such an attempt was necessary and inevitable. The idea of the unity of the world had dominated all the political doctrines of the Middle Ages, the constitution of a Universal State—the only State of which the Middle Ages had, in general, any conception—having been regarded as the absolute good in itself and as the essential condition of universal peace. The sovereignty of that State had been resumed by the civilians in the Empire, on the basis of the civil law; by the canonists in the Roman Church, on the basis of the canon law; and, when Empire and Church existed as separate powers, there arose the doctrine of the Pope as vicar of God, the Lord of Heaven, and the emperor as regent of God, the Lord of the earth. Then, the Church having survived the Empire and ultimately lost its supremacy with the loss of its moral authority, another foundation for the world-unity—which ideal still persisted—had to be found. And it was found in Natural Law.

Thus human reason, right reason, becomes the basis of the laws and institutions of society. It is for man to discover and apply, in Natural Law, the Divine Law. But though it is within the field of his own essential nature that man, aided by reason, must carry on this search, yet necessity, the voice of Nature, may, on occasion, be the only determinant. So Grotius claims—and to this extent, though not as absolute pioneer, he may be said to have separated jurisprudence from theology—that his theory would have been equally valid even if the existence of God were not conceded. And thus the jurists of the school of Grotius are not fast-bound to the idea of the supremacy of either Church or Empire or even of the Divine Law. The principle of the sociability and solidarity of independent States—not necessarily equal, however—founded on the interests of humanity at large and discoverable and applicable by human reason, is the foundation of their science, the characteristic of what is generally known as Protestant thought.

That which is left after this Natural Law is exhausted may—according to Grotius—be the subject of positive law, either Divine or human. And it is only subject to the provisions of Divine positive law that human positive law, that is to say, civil (municipal) law and *jus gentium* (the Law of Nations) is possible. But the Law of Nations is rarely to be found, it must be noted, apart or even distinguishable from Natural Law, and is, apparently, nothing but Natural Law itself in one of its aspects. It may, it would seem, be an expression of Attributive Justice, or moral right, or even an application in practice of any of the cardinal virtues—not only of Justice, but also, as they may be applicable, of temperance, courage, wisdom or charity. Utility, however, though at once the occasion and the sanction of human positive law whether civil or *jus gentium*, is not its source or impulse. More precisely—though Grotius is far from being generally consistent—*jus gentium* is that common human law which derives its authority from the unanimous approbation of all, or at least many, nations, but which, nevertheless, may differ in various parts of the world, though always evidenced, like the unwritten civil law, by continued use and the testimony of men skilled in the law. What real difference, there is between *jus gentium* and Natural Law is that, while the former is derived, like the latter, from the principles of nature, yet it evolves, generally quite indistinguishable from Natural Law, only in the social relations introduced by that deterioration of human nature which was caused by the Fall of Man. And *jus gentium* may be distinguished, too, from the civil law—the former does not respect the advantage of any particular societies but of all in general. So " wise kings regard themselves as entrusted with the care of not one nation only but of all mankind."

This conception of *jus gentium* is obviously very different from that of the Roman law. And Grotius himself seems to suggest that his Roman prototype is rather the fecial law. The true *jus gentium*, that of Rome, was municipal law, and not *jus inter gentes*—international law in the modern sense. It was composed of those principles and rules of private and public law which Rome, recognising them as being equally observed by, and in that sense common to, all peoples, herself applied in relation to matters outside the operation of the *jus civile*, as, for instance, in her dealings with other nations and in litigation between non-Romans and between Romans and non-Romans. The jurists of the Middle Ages, however, and, indeed, the more immediate precursors of Grotius, had no such conception of it.

It is said that the Grotian *jus gentium* was a return to that of St. Isidore of Seville; but that can hardly be the case. Though St. Isidore, leaving Natural Law entirely on one side, divides human or positive law into civil law and *jus gentium*, yet he does not define *jus gentium* (b). Instead, he enumerates twelve juridical topics, all of which—such as occupation of territory, war, treaties—belong or might belong to any system of *jus inter gentes*, or international law proper. And these topics are of *jus gentium* because the rules in relation to them are the same among nearly all peoples. *Jus gentium*, according to St. Isidore—who, it should be observed, writes not as a jurist but merely as an encyclopædic compiler, his one object being to place upon record only generally accepted contemporary doctrine—does not, therefore, proceed so much from first principles and theory to particular rules as from a practical desire

---

(b) St. Isidore also has a *jus militare*, which is a general military law, only merely procedural, apparently, when dealing with matters subject to *jus gentium*.

to bring under one head certain existing social conditions of an exceptional yet characteristic class.   Gratian, five centuries afterwards, does no more than faithfully reproduce St. Isidore, designing thereby only to declare the law as it was then generally received and not to make it.   But with the coming of scholasticism and the revival of jurisprudence this position was abandoned.   At the same time there is an end of consistency and certainty.   Nor is this surprising when the development of the theory is found to lie in the hands of four separate schools—each anxious to create for itself some characteristic doctrine—the civilians and the canonists, and the theologians who found their main inspiration in patristic philosophy, and the philosophers whose great authority was classical thought.   Azo teaches that *jus gentium* is nothing else than that law which is observed by all peoples, as distinguished from all animals, and, subject to that distinction, is identical with Natural Law.   It arises, apparently, only when social relationships have been established between men, and comprehends those rights which society necessarily involves, *e.g.* of religion, the person, child-nurture, family order, preservation and delimitation of property and national territory, and, in general, contract, and also, incidentally, war.   And Bracton, emphasising regal privilege, closely follows Azo.   With St. Thomas Aquinas, however, who " drew the great outlines for the following centuries," *jus gentium* is deprived of almost everything precise and objective, and becomes entirely speculative, as a result of a philosophical effort, concentrating upon first principles and theory, devoted to placing it in a definite relation to or association with Natural Law.   To *jus gentium*—it now appears—belong those things which are derived from Natural Law, " as conclusions from premisses, *e.g.* just buyings and sellings, and the like," without which men cannot live together, " which is a point of nature," since man is by nature a social animal, while those things which are derived from Natural Law " by way of particular determination," belong to the civil law, according as each State decides on what is best for itself.   And then, in the following century, while we find Bartolus apparently quite indifferent to *jus gentium* as such, save, perhaps, for some incidental recognition of its relation to such matters as territorial divisions and regal power, Legnano carefully identifies it with natural equity—the bare general equity of natural intelli-

gence. War, however, according to Legnano, arises from Natural
Law as distinguished from *jus gentium*, which only regulates it.
At about the same period—such is the confusion—while the
Lombard enactments are, on occasion, styled *jus gentium* when
compared with the Roman Law—the general or common law of
Europe—it is being argued that the Italian municipal codes
should take precedence of the Roman Law for the reason that
the latter is only *jus gentium*. If we pass over another century
we reach a period when jurists—Valla, Conanus—who, like Azo,
do not agree that brutes come within Natural Law, are to be
found denying that *jus gentium* can be distinguished at all from
Natural Law. Soto—*qui scit Sotum scit totum* is the contemporary jingle—has been classed with these, but he has also been
interpreted as teaching that while Natural Law is apprehended
without human effort because of the dictates of Nature, *jus gentium*
is a living body of examples and precedents—the contribution of
all peoples—whose precepts or lesson can be known, though only
with difficulty, and should be followed, by pagans equally with
Christians. Other jurists, Budaeus and Oldendorp, for instance,
teach simply that *jus gentium* is that which is common to all
men, that is, received everywhere as law. It is the authority of
men rather than that of Nature. It is the law of many peoples,
just as the civil law is the law of the individual. And Cujas holds
that it is natural equity, common to all mankind—born with us
and known to all. So we reach a period immediately preceding
that of Grotius. To Ayala Natural Law is the law of that "blame-
less primitive time" which "pagans used to call the Golden Age,"
when all things were in common and nothing belonged to any
individual, *jus gentium* having its origin in the succeeding age,
when primitive conditions were no longer adapted to man's
"debased nature," developing, under the guidance of natural
reason, with the new and increasingly complex society. Gentilis,
Protestant and founder of modern International Law, makes no
pretence at being a philosopher, or at being versed in the subtleties
of the schools, whether theological or juridical. He has the
appearance of being only a plain and practical lawyer. He notices
only two of the prevailing theories of *jus gentium*, and specifically
adopts neither. One is that which assigns to it those laws, based
on reason, common to most peoples, and identifies it with Natural

Law, and the other is that which attributes to it the common God-given unwritten law of mankind, found in the human heart or nature rather than instituted by reason. For himself, without actually repudiating either of these theories, he is content to search the writings of the philosophers and even the poets of antiquity—for are not their views based upon observation and experience?—the Scriptures and the Fathers, the civil law and history and political literature. In such manner he may discover a common law of nations. This position is not far from that of Suarez, the philosopher of the schools. Philosophically, *jus gentium* is to him an equivocal expression, suggesting, at best, something lying almost indeterminate between Natural Law and human law and partaking of the character of each. Practically regarded, however, it is Divine Law and the common usage of mankind interpreted in the light of reason. And it is to be found in two relations. In the one it is that law which obtains within a political society—its common law—and is substantially identical with a similar law to be found in all, or nearly all, other such societies. It is thus the common private law of the world, and thus, in effect, only an aspect of Natural Law. But in the other relation it is that law which all political societies must observe in their intercourse one with the other. Mankind, according to Suarez—and here he falls into line with the idea of the heterodox Ockham—has a certain unity, though actually divided into various peoples and States. And this unity is not only " specific " but also " quasi-political and moral." No such people or State, however perfect it may be in itself and homogeneous in its constituents, is altogether self-sufficient and independent, but, on the contrary, has an inherent need of the help and society of, and intercourse with, other peoples or States. A State, like a man, is a social being. Hence the need and existence of rules of law as between political societies; and these rules, *jus gentium*, are to be gathered from international usage and tradition.

So it appears that the very concrete conception of *jus gentium* of St. Isidore had disappeared centuries before the day of Grotius, giving place to a highly abstract and speculative doctrine so subtle and vague—if, indeed, we can extract it at all from the foregoing very inadequate summary—that the generations of scholastic theologians and jurists who undertook to define and develop it only rendered it the more obscure and uncertain the more they discussed it. And it is this scholastic doctrine—and certainly not the *jus gentium* of Rome—that Grotius adopts, his version varying from those, or any of those, of his precursors much, generally, as their versions had varied as between themselves.

Only slightly more definitely than his precursors could Grotius escape the domination of the idea that the main relation of *jus gentium* was to " corporeal bodies "—individual men; rather than —to use the expression of Legnano—to those " mystic bodies," societies or States. Nor can he, when dealing with first principles, distinguish it with certainty from Natural Law, which so frequently in his great work, even in connections where *jus gentium* might be expected to reign supreme, thrusts that law aside and itself almost exclusively commands the situation. Thus, when discussing that most important question, whether war can ever be lawful, Grotius deals first and at length with Natural Law, and then, in but a few sentences, with *jus gentium*, which, he says, may be but another name for Natural Law. So, declining the teaching of the Roman Law and firm in the view that slavery involves nothing inconsistent with natural justice, he justifies and founds that condition by and on Natural Law—in this case a very exiguous conception—and not *jus gentium*. Then, as for the place he assigns to human reason, the scholastics assigned the same. Human reason, according to St. Thomas, is nothing else than an imprint on us of the Divine light, or rather—as he also puts it— man has a share of the Eternal Reason, whereby he has a natural inclination to his proper act and end, such participation of the eternal law in the rational creature being called the Natural Law. And this is the doctrine of the Thomists down to and including Suarez. And thus only most vaguely are Natural Law and human law dependent upon the Divine Law.

Where, then, does the system of the *De Jure Belli* substantially differ from that of its predecessors? Shortly in this, that the jurisprudence of the scholastics begins and ends with general principles, discussed, almost always, most abstractly, while that of Grotius, beginning with the same general principles so discussed, yet proceeds at once to its conclusions through a most comprehensive and systematic body of particular and concrete illustration. We say illustration—and herein is a signal defect in the method of

Grotius—for, notwithstanding such difference, he seems to be living in and writing for the ancient world rather than in and for the world of his day. Unlike others, as Gentilis, who were then opening up the same ground—or even Ayala—he has no concern whatever for contemporary or recent precedent. A fable from classical mythology is more to him than an incident in the' international relations of the Dutch. But nevertheless his association in one system of the practical with the merely theoretical was a striking and important achievement, and largely explains the influence his work was destined to exert.

It is therefore no redundance that the full title of this work is more extensive in its suggestion than that of its first and best-known part, *De Jure Belli*. This must not only always be read with the *ac Pacis*, but also as introductory to the rest—*including the Law of Nature and of Nations and the Principal Points of Public Law*. The work is really a practical treatise on Natural Law. It is that law, as interpreted and supported, where possible, by positive Divine Law—which supplies its foundation and inspires its main propositions. Except in relation to the obvious, the Law of Nations is nothing else than Natural Law.

But of the whole work only a small part, and that at the opening, is devoted to general theory. About a half of the remainder is a discussion of municipal law, public and private. This, while professedly a deduction from Natural Law and *jus gentium* elaborated to smallest details, is actually an exposition of Roman Law and a bold application of its principles to international relations in certain particular matters, as, for instance, newly-discovered territory, diplomacy, and treaties; and the work concludes with a system of law of war indistinguishable in the main from the work of his predecessors. But it is that detailed exposition of municipal law, public and private—at once an apparent deduction from Natural Law, and also a point of departure for developing the laws of international relations and war—that determined the great influence of the work. Henceforth Natural Law was not only the warrant for municipal law, but also, through or in the latter—public and private rights being barely distinguished—the apparent foundation for a practical system of International Law. So, amongst many other principles, *usucapio* and prescription are applied to the relations of Sovereigns and States, the rights of a landowner to those of a King, and the doctrine of justifiable homicide to the problem of war. And Western civilisation having the future it did, there was but one possible future for this book. The work of a Protestant, so modern, popular, and convenient in method and form, it must supplant the less comprehensive work of Gentilis, and render henceforth unnecessary the elaborate and interminable *a priori* efforts of Suarez and his predecessors of the schools.

The learning of these, his precursors, had not been surpassed, nor had it hardly been approached. Nor was there a more perfect dialectic, a greater breadth of vision, or a deeper humanism or warmer charity to be found in this newcomer into the field of juridical literature. It was that Europe, with feudalism in its death-throes and Church and Empire riven asunder, had urgent need of a general theory of the State, of the nation, and its organisation. The contractual theory of government was now rising out of the dissolving feudal system, and here was Grotius frankly developing that theory by a bold assimilation of public powers to private rights. So it was the general course·of events, the very atmosphere of a rapidly changing and developing Europe, that determined the reputation and influence that the *De Jure Belli* was to enjoy and to command.

Wherever justice is established, there, in the resulting unity, peace will inevitably be found. That—it must not be overlooked —is the one principle that above all others breathes throughout the work. It is not especially Grotian, though, for it can be found as a dominant influence throughout the long length of classical and mediæval political thought. St. Augustine, adopting Cicero's definition of a republic, had long before stereotyped the idea for the scholastics. It is, however, the principle that in the hands of Grotius was to suggest the great part which the notion of contract could play in any system of international right. According to Grotius, every political society is based upon contract between its members, the first contract of all, one, simply declaratory of the law of nature, by which its members emerge from the state of nature. These members, too, move amongst themselves within their society by contract. So can and should move all the political societies within the great human society;

for the plan of the world includes societies or States, as well as individuals or citizens, with all the relative inequalities of the latter, and contract involves the idea of the right, of justice, and always of obligation and good faith. Wherever, therefore, in international affairs there is an absence of contract, or, there being contract, justice is wanting and bad faith prevails, anarchy or war alone will exist. It is this theory in particular, involving, as it does, the fundamental conception of Natural Law, that makes the transition from the mediæval to the modern point of view.

So Grotius may be said to be a pacifist, but only in theory and with peace as no more than ideal. At best he is merely partizan of peace—the advocate of peace because of its general expediency. His theory is simply an advocate's argument; and if by peace we are to understand an era of perpetual peace, it is difficult to regard Grotius as having at any time even barely considered its possibility. He himself was not in the slightest degree a pacifist in relation to his personal interests. As poet he sang the glories as well as the horrors of war—on rare occasion his muse almost inspired; as historian, though often depicting its miseries, he never stigmatised it generally as essentially unjust or inexpedient; as politician and diplomatist he would have had recourse to war for no other cause than that it might further his particular policy; as jurist and philosopher his sole great concern was that war should be waged only for just cause and as a last resort, and then only lawfully; and as theologian he never forgot that just warfare, as an institution, was divinely approved.

The key to the position of Grotius is to be found in the dedicatory epistle addressed to Louis XIII. It is Louis " the Just " to whom he insistently appeals that Justice may enter into her own in international affairs, and Peace, obviously only in relation to the existing wars, then reign throughout Christendom as long as possible. The aim of Grotius is to develop and insist upon the idea of justice. So let there be an era of international contract and good faith; and then, with princes satisfied as to the moral and material expediency of peace, and determined not to resort to arms save reluctantly and for undoubted good cause, even the widest international differences may perhaps be composed, if not by the parties themselves, by mediators, arbitrators, or even international congresses. So war may become less and less frequent, and, if regard be had to his rules, less horrible.

Grotius was forty-two years of age when he published the *De Jure Belli*; and having published it, he immediately turns his attention to other interests and projects without any real idea that he had already accomplished that which was to be his most enduring monument. This, his latest effort, had not even suggested specialisation on the same lines. His ambition, keen as ever, was of the same indeterminate, restless, and eclectic character as before. Though his reputation as jurist was now established, his interest in legal science seems very largely to have disappeared. He would now, as in his earlier years, be poet, philologist, scholar, and theologian, and, in particular, protagonist of religious peace. But to live he must find some occupation of profit, and it was to diplomacy that he turned.

For some years he sought an opening. In 1635 he was appointed ambassador of Sweden in Paris; and so he finds himself settled in France in a definite and distinguished position, and occupied with work that best appealed to him. As representative of the chief actor with France in the Thirty Years' War, it might be his task to negotiate the peace that must one day come. But on his diplomatic activities we have no space to dwell. Shortly, they are a chapter in the usual tale of political dispute, intrigue, and negotiation incident to a "world-war." Grotius seems to have played his part honestly, and generally to the satisfaction of his principals, but at the same time without quite all the tact and finesse desirable. Doubtless his soul was in his study, and the intellectual society of which Paris was then the centre and in which he occupied a distinguished position. He was continuously at work in the field of scholarship and history. His separately published works number ninety-five altogether, of which no fewer than four hundred and sixty-two editions and translations are known. He completed, amongst other works, an enormous critical commentary, or *Annotationes*, on the Scriptures, a labour of great philological, exegetical, and historical value, which placed him in the ranks of the pioneers of the higher criticism. His one great pre-occupation, however, was the reunion of the Churches. He remained throughout his life a member of the Reformed Church, but his sympathies gradually so widened in relation to

discipline and ritual as to embrace a strong inclination towards
episcopal and even Roman Catholicism. Perhaps the Anglicanism
of Bishop Andrewes was the ecclesiastical system that most
appealed to him, and there is no doubt that in the Anglican Church
he saw the nucleus of any possible reunion. But his doctrinal
standpoint was always indefinite. While, on the one hand, he
retained in principle a profound faith in revelation, he yet, on the
other, adopted a critico-historical and rationalistic style of treatment which would seem to be hardly consistent with the existence
of that faith if we overlook the essential rationalism of Scholasticism, and, indeed, of Catholicism itself.

It is, however, in the light of its author's undoubted bias—faith
in revelation—that, notwithstanding its formal · rationalism,
the *De Jure Belli* must be read and can alone be appreciated.
Grotius was the boy who, pupil of Uytenbogart and Francis
Junius, had undertaken the conversion of his mother, the young
man who, inclining toward literature, had composed the *Christus
Patiens* and the *Adamus Exul* and a whole volume of minor sacred
and devotional verse, and who, throwing himself into public life,
became champion of Arminianism, and strove, even with Kings,
to further the great cause of Christian reunion and peace. His
career checked and diverted by political chance, he yet remains
throughout his life devotedly faithful to his first and greatest
call. As in his earlier years he wrote a juridical work, the *De Jure
Praedae*, including in that his famous *Mare Liberum*, because
of the need of answer to the Mennonite theology, so in his maturity
he gave to the world the *De Jure Belli* as the protest of a true
believer—only incidentally a jurist—against the increasing lust of
political Christendom for lawless and unconscionable war. Then,
save for the time he must of necessity devote to the immediately
practical interests of life, and some time he found, as for recreation,
for literature and scholarship, he returns once for all to matters
theological and ecclesiastical. His interest in the *De Jure Belli*
and its destiny is but the slightest. His one dominating thought
is religion—the Scriptures and the Church. His one ambition—
to help forward the cause of religious peace by and through a
reunited Church.

In 1645 he was at Stockholm, resigning his diplomatic appoint-
ment. Returning in August, he takes ship for Lübeck, but storms

force a landing at Danzig. Weather-beaten and ill, making his way overland, he reaches Rostock, too feeble to journey further. In three days' time, on the 29th, his ardent, restless spirit at length found the Unity where there shall be no more war; and on earth, for generations, men were to dispute whether he had died Protestant or Romanist. As a fact he died a Christian only, though formally in the Reformed Faith.

BIBLIOGRAPHY.

De Jure Belli ac Pacis. 1 vol. Paris. 1625. Edit. prin.

De Jure Belli et Pacis. Accompanied by an abridged translation by W. Whewell. 3 vols. London. 1853.

De Jure Belli ac Pacis. Edited by P. C. Molhuysen. 1 vol. Leyden. 1919.

The Rights of War and Peace. A translation of the *De Jure Belli* by " Several Hands." 3 vols. London. 1715.

The Rights of War and Peace. An abridged translation by W. Whewell. 1 vol. London. 1853.

Le droit de la guerre et de la paix. Traduction par Jean Barbeyrac. 2 vols. Amsterdam. 1724.

Le droit de la guerre et de la paix. Traduction par M. P. Pradier-Fodéré. 3 vols. Paris. 1867.

De Jure Praedae. 1 vol. The Hague. 1868.

Mare Liberum. Translated with a revision of the Latin text of 1633 by Ralph Van Deman Magoffin. 1 vol. New York. 1916.

Vie de Grotius. Par Levesque de Burigny. 2 vols. Paris. 1752. 2 vols. Amsterdam. 1754.

Life of Grotius. Translated from Levesque de Burigny. 1 vol. London. 1754.

Life of Grotius. By Chas. Butler. London. 1826.

Etude sur la vie et les travaux de Grotius. Par A. Caumont. Paris. 1862.

Etude sur le "droit de la guerre" de Grotius. Par V. Hely. Paris. 1875.

Le droit de la guerre et les précurseurs de Grotius. Par E. Nys. Bruxelles. 1882.

Les Fondateurs du Droit International. Ed. par A. Pillet (Grotius, par Jules Basdevant). Paris. 1904.

Seven Great Statesmen. By Andrew D. White. London. 1910.

Le droit de guerre d'après les théologiens et les canonistes du moyen-age. Par A. Vanderpol. Paris. 1911.

La Guerre devant le Christianisme. Par A. Vanderpol. Paris. 1912.

La doctrine scolastique du droit de guerre. Par A. Vanderpol. Paris. 1919.

Collected Papers of John Westlake on Public International Law. Cambridge. 1914.

Hugo Grotius. By Hamilton Vreeland, jun. New York. 1917.

The Influence of Grotius. By Sir John Macdonell (Transactions, Grotius Society, Vol. V.). London. 1920.

Grotius in England. By W. S. M. Knight (Transactions, Grotius Society, Vol. V.). London. 1920.

Hugo Grotius: His Family and Ancestry. By W. S. M. Knight (Transactions, Grotius Society, Vol. VI.). London. 1921.

Hugo Grotius: His Infancy and Youth. By W. S. M. Knight (Transactions, Grotius Society, Vol. VII.). London. 1922.

SELECTIONS FROM THREE BOOKS
ON
THE RIGHTS OF WAR AND PEACE
INCLUDING THE LAW OF NATURE AND OF NATIONS,
AND THE PRINCIPAL POINTS OF PUBLIC LAW.

BOOK III.

PROLEGOMENA.

1. Many have undertaken to explain or summarize, either by commentaries or abridgments, the civil law of Rome and other nations; but few have dealt with that law which exists between several peoples or rulers of peoples, whether it be that derived from Nature herself or instituted by Divine decrees or created by custom and tacit agreement; and no one at all has so far discussed it generally and in systematic fashion, although it is of importance to mankind that this should be done.

2. Rightly indeed has Cicero called this a pre-eminent science, including as it does the alliances, treaties, and stipulations of peoples, kings, and foreign nations, and, in short, the whole law of war and peace. And Euripides gives to this science precedence even before a knowledge of things divine and human, and so makes Helen thus speak to Theone: "It would be disgraceful that you should know the present and future of men and gods, and yet not know what justice is."

3. And the more necessary is this work inasmuch as in both our own and past time there are not, and have not been, wanting those who have despised this branch of law as though it were nothing more than merely. an empty name. The words of Euphemus, according to Thucydides, that " a king, or a State, can do nothing unjust when acting in his or its own interest," are in almost everyone's mouth; and to this may be added the like saying, that " for those who enjoy supreme power the right is on the side of the power." Again, " A State cannot be preserved without inflicting some injury." And, let us add, the disputes that arise between peoples or kings usually have Mars as arbiter. Nor is it the opinion only of the common people that war is a stranger to all justice; for words often fall from learned and judicious men which support the same idea. Nothing indeed is

more frequent than placing law and arms in opposition to each other. Ennius, for instance, has said: "They gain their right by force of arms, not by law." And Horace thus describes the fierceness of Achilles: "Law he spurns as not for him existing, and claims all by arms"; and another poet introduces another warrior, when beginning a war, as saying: "Now I renounce peace and violate laws." Antigonus, though old, laughed at a man who offered him a treatise on justice at a time when he was laying siege to some towns that did not belong to him. And Marius said he could not hear the voice of the laws because of the clash of arms. Even the modest Pompey had the effrontery to say: "Am I, who am armed, to think of laws?"

4. In the Christian writers occur many passages in the same sense; let one from Tertullian suffice for all: "Fraud, cruelty, injustice, are the proper business of battles." Now those who are of this opinion will undoubtedly oppose to me that of Terence: "You that attempt to fix by certain rules things so uncertain, may with like success strive to go mad and yet preserve your reason."

5. But since a discourse upon this kind of law would be vain if in fact there were no such law, then, at once as recommendation and defence of our work, it will be necessary briefly to refute this most gross error; and that we may not have to deal with a mob of opponents, let us assign to them an advocate. And who better than Carneades, who attained such perfection in what was the supreme aim of his philosophical school that he could argue with the full force of his eloquence no less easily in favour of the false than for the truth? He, when he undertook to argue against justice, and especially that part of it with which we are now concerned, found no stronger contention than this: Laws were instituted by men as their own advantage suggested, he urges, different as their customs differed, and even in the same society frequently changing with the times; and so there is no such thing as Natural Law. For all men and other living creatures are moved by Nature towards their own interests; and so either there is no justice at all, or, if there be any, it is supreme folly, inasmuch as in consulting the interests of others it injures itself.

6. But one certainly ought not to grant what the philosopher here says and the poet adopts: "Nature cannot distinguish

between the just and the unjust." For though man is certainly
a living creature, yet he is an extraordinary one, differing, as he
does, much more from all other kinds of animals than these do
amongst themselves; a fact which is proved by the many faculties
characteristic of mankind. Now one of the most striking of these
faculties is man's desire for society, that is, for a life, peaceable
and not spent anyhow, of association with those of his own kind,
ordered in manner appropriate to his intelligence—a desire termed
by the Stoics the domestic instinct. So one should not concede
the proposition when applied so generally—that Nature leads
every creature to seek only its own interests.

8. This guarding of society which we have now but roughly
described, consonant as it is to human intelligence, is the very
spring of that law, properly so called, to which belong the following
rules—that one must abstain from that which belongs to another;
that one must restore that which one holds and which belongs
to another, or the profit made thereout; that promises must be
fulfilled; that reparation must be made for the consequences of
wrongdoing; and that the punishment of a man may be deserved.

9. And from this signification of law proceeds another yet more
extensive. Man, above all other creatures, enjoys not only this
social faculty of which we have just spoken, but also judgment
to decide what actions are to his advantage or are harmful to
him not only at the moment but in the future, and even the
consequences resulting therefrom. Hence it may be concluded
that it is conformable to human nature to follow in these matters
a judgment rightly formed, regard being had to the limitations of
the human mind, and not be misled either by fear or by the
temptation of present advantage or be carried away by reckless
impulse. Whatever, indeed, is obviously repugnant to such a
judgment is also contrary to Natural Law, that is to say, to the
Law of Human Nature.

10. And here we meet with the question of the exercise of wise
discretion in the distribution to each individual or body of men
of that which should be his or theirs; so that in some cases the
wiser man is preferred to the less wise, a neighbour to a stranger,
or a poor man to a rich, according as the merit of each act or the
nature of the thing requires. Many authors, indeed, both ancient
and modern, regard this as within the province of law properly

so called, notwithstanding such law has a very different nature, restricted as it is to permitting what belongs to another to be left with him or requiring what is his due to be paid.

12. Now we come to another origin of law, besides that of Nature, namely, the free will of God, to which, as our understanding infallibly dictates, we must be subject. . . .

13. . . . God, by the laws which He has given, has rendered these principles more clear and evident, even to those whose minds are less capable of strict reasoning. And He has also forbidden submission to those reckless impulses which, contrary to our own and others' good, prevent us observing the rules of reason and Nature; and thus does He control and restrain, within certain limits, our more violent passions.

15. Again, since it is by Natural Law that compacts are to be observed (because it was necessary that there should be some means by which men could be bound to one another, and no other natural mode can be imagined), it is from that same source that civil laws are derived; for those who had united themselves with any society, or subjected themselves to any man or men, either expressly promised, or from the nature of the case must be understood tacitly to have promised, that they would conform to whatever should be ordained either by the majority of the society or by those in whom authority was vested.

16. Therefore, that is untrue, if we speak accurately, which not only Carneades, but others, have said, that " Utility is the mother of the Just and the Right." For the mother of Natural Law is human nature itself, which would create in us a desire for mutual society even though our necessities should have no actual need of it. And the mother of civil law is that very obligation which arises from consent, and which, deriving its force from Natural Law, makes it permissible to term Nature the grandmother, as it were, of civil law. But utility is added to Natural Law; because the Author of Nature willed that we should be weak as individuals, and yet need many of the necessities of a complete life, so that we might the more eagerly desire the social life. Of civil law, however, utility is but the occasion; for that association or subjection of which we have spoken began just for the sake of some utility. So they who prescribe laws for others usually aim, or ought to aim, at some utility therein.

17. But as the laws of each community have in view the utility or advantage of that community, so between all or most communities some laws might be, and in fact are, established by consent, which aim at the utility not only of some particular community but of the whole in general. This is what is called the Law of Nations, as distinguished from Natural Law. And this part of law was omitted by Carneades, when dividing all law into Natural Law and the civil law of particular communities, notwithstanding he most certainly ought to have referred to it inasmuch as he was about to treat of the law between peoples—in fact, he proceeds with a discourse about war and acquisition by war.

18. And quite absurdly has Carneades traduced justice as folly; for since, by his own admission, that citizen is not a fool who obeys the law of his country, even though he consequently loses something to his advantage, so, therefore, that people is not foolish that for the sake of its own advantage does not disregard the laws common to all peoples. The principle is the same in each case. Inasmuch, indeed, as he who breaks the laws of his country for the sake of some present personal advantage thereby destroys that which secures the perpetual advantage of himself and his posterity, so, too, the people that violates the laws of nature and of nations breaks down the safeguards of its present and future peace. Moreover, even if no advantage were to be expected from the observance of law, yet it would be a point of wisdom, not of folly, to obey the impulse and direction of our own nature.

19. So, that other opinion is not universally true: " 'Twas fear of wrong that made us make our laws "—which a disputant in one of Plato's Dialogues explains as meaning that the fear of receiving injury occasioned the invention of laws, and that it was by force that men were driven to the practice of justice. For this view has validity only in relation to those institutions and laws which were devised in order to facilitate the execution of justice. Thus, when many, individually feeble, lest they be oppressed by the stronger, combine to establish and maintain judicial institutions by their common strength, in order jointly to control those whom they, as individuals, could not deal with. In this sense we can even fairly accept what is elsewhere said in Plato, that law is that which pleases the stronger, understanding thereby, however,

that law fails to attain its external end unless it has the aid of
force. Thus Solon accomplished very great things, as he himself
claimed, " By linking Force in the same yoke with Law."

20. Yet law does not lose all its effect, even though deprived
of the aid of force. For justice brings repose to the conscience;
injustice torture and remorse, such as Plato describes as dwelling
in the breasts of tyrants. The general consent of the upright,
too, approves justice and condemns injustice. But what is the
greatest point of all is that God is the Friend of justice and the
Enemy of injustice, and reserves His judgments for a future life,
though in such manner that He often manifests their power in
this life, as history teaches by many examples.

21. There are many who, while they demand respect for justice
in private citizens, regard it as unnecessary in nations and rulers
of nations. This is wrong. The reason of the error is, primarily,
that such people have regard for nothing in law other than the
advantage arising from it, and which advantage is obvious in the
case of private citizens, who, separately, are too weak to protect
themselves. But great States, which seem to contain within
themselves everything necessary for the maintenance of their
well-being, have apparently no need of that virtue which respects
the interests of others and is called justice.

22. But, not to repeat what I have already said, namely, that
law was not instituted for the sake of utility alone, there is no
State so strong but that sometimes it may need the assistance of
others, either in commerce, or to repel the aggression of the combined forces of many foreign nations. Hence we see that alliances
are desired even by the most powerful nations and kings; the whole
principle of which is undermined by those who confine the operation of law within the limits of one State only. Most true is it,
indeed, that everything is dissolved into uncertainty the moment
the conception of law disappears.

23. If there is no society that can subsist without law, as
Aristotle proved by the striking example of a band of robbers,
then, certainly, law cannot be ignored by that society which is
composed of all mankind, or, at least, a number of nations. . . .

25. There are people who teach that all laws cease in war.
This, however, cannot be admitted. Rather, no war should be
commenced except for the assertion of the right, or be carried on

except according to the measure of law and good faith. Demosthenes sensibly said that it is against those who refuse to be bound by judicial decree that war is rightly waged. For judgments have force against those who are sensible of their inability to resist them. Wars are the remedy against those who make, or think, themselves the equal of the judicial authority. Yet nevertheless, in order that warlike proceedings may be right, they must be carried out as conscientiously as judgments are accustomed to be executed.

26. So, therefore, only those laws that are civil and judicial and proper to times of peace, are silent amidst the clash of arms; but not those other laws that are perpetual and equally proper at all times. For, as Dio Prusæensis so very well said : " Written, that is to say, civil laws, have no force as between belligerents, but those laws are valid that are unwritten, that is to say, are dictated by nature or instituted by the consent of nations. . . ."

28. Now, being thus fully convinced, on the grounds I have just adduced, that there is some law common to all nations which applies both to the initiation of war and to the manner in which war should be carried on, there were many and weighty considerations impelling me to write a treatise on the subject of that law. I observed everywhere in Christendom a lawlessness in warfare of which even barbarous nations would be ashamed. Nations would rush to arms on the slightest pretext or even without cause at all. And arms once taken up, there would be an end to all respect for law, whether human or divine, as though a fury had been let loose with general licence for all manner of crime.

29. And the spectacle of this monstrous barbarity has led many men—in no wise extremists—to the opinion that all arms should be forbidden a Christian, whose rule of life is mainly the loving of all men. Those ardent lovers of peace, both ecclesiastical and civil, John Ferus and our countryman Erasmus, seem sometimes to incline to this opinion, though I believe that they do so on the principle that to straighten a bent stick one must bend it strongly the other way. But this attempt to force too much to an opposite extreme often does more harm than good, inasmuch as exaggeration, so readily apparent, detracts from the authority of a more reasonably advanced truth. A remedy must therefore be found for both schools of extremists—for those that believe

that in war nothing is lawful and for those for whom all things are lawful in war.

30. Moreover, I was anxious, by my private efforts, to promote the study and authority of jurisprudence, which I had formerly practised in public offices with all possible integrity; for this, indeed, is all that I can now undertake, having been shamefully banished from my native country, distinguished though it was by so many of my labours. Many, hitherto, have aimed at a scientific treatment of the subject, but no one has yet succeeded. Nor, indeed, is success possible, unless care be taken where, so far, there has been insufficient care, namely, in the strict separation of laws arising out of human compact from those derived from nature. These latter, being always the same, can easily be brought together in a system; but the former, which depend upon the human will, and so often change, and differ in different places, are outside the scope of scientific treatment, just as are other ideas of particular things.

31. But if the exponents of true justice would undertake the treatment of the several parts of that jurisprudence which is natural and perpetual, putting aside all derived from the free will of man, so that, for instance, one would treat of laws, another of tributes, another of the duties of judges, another of the ascertainment of intention, and another of evidence as to facts, we might eventually, by collecting all its parts, construct a *corpus* of such jurisprudence.

BOOK I.

CHAPTER I.—WHAT WAR IS, AND WHAT RIGHT IS.

I. The disputes of those who are not bound by one common civil law, such as people who have not yet been incorporated into a State, have relation either to times of war or times of peace. So, too, the controversies of those, whether private persons or kings, who belong to different States. And so the differences of those who enjoy a sovereign power, such as, in a constitutional State, an aristocratic senate or even a popular assembly. But because war is waged with a view to peace, and there is no dispute whence war cannot spring, all disputes which usually arise are rightly treated under the head of the law of war. So war will lead us to peace, as its end and aim.

II. (1) Having therefore to treat of the law of war, we must discover what that war is with which we are concerned and what that law is which we seek. Cicero has called war "a dispute by force." But custom has ruled that it is not the act, but the status, or condition, that is indicated by the word "war," so that war is the status of those who so dispute. And in this general sense the term comprehends all those kinds of war which will be presently discussed, not even excluding private war, which is really more ancient than public war, with which it has, without doubt, a common nature, and so may have the same proper name. . . . (3) . . . We do not include justice in the definition, for that is precisely the point we are to discuss in this work—whether any war can be just and what war is actually just. But we must distinguish the subject of our discussion, "War," from what we discuss in relation to it.

III. (1) In entitling this work "The Rights of War," we regard as of first importance the problem we have just posed: Can any war be just, and, if so, what war is just? For in this connection "law" is to be taken in the sense of "right," or, to put it negatively rather than affirmatively, "law" or the "lawful, ' the "just" or the "right," is that which is "not unjust" or is not wrong. Now that is unjust which is repugnant to the nature of a rational society. So, as Cicero says, it is against nature to take from another to enrich oneself; and then he proves it by showing that if that were not so human society would necessarily be destroyed. . . . (2) But as there are some societies without inequality, as among brothers, citizens, friends, and allies, and some unequal—according to their respective excellency, as Aristotle terms it—as the relation between father and children, master and servant, king and subject, and God and man, so there is the one justice of those who have equality among themselves and the other of the ruler and the ruled. And we rightly call, if I am not mistaken, that of the latter class the Right of Superiority and the former the Right of Equality.

IV. There is, however, another and different meaning to the Right, or Justice, though derived from the same source, which may be referred to persons. In this sense the just is the moral quality of an individual capable of having or doing something justly. This right belongs to a person, though sometimes it relates to a thing, as in the case of a praedial servitude, when it is called a real right, as compared to one exclusively personal. This is not because a person has the thing, but because no one else has the right than he who has the thing itself. This moral quality, when perfect, is called by us a faculty. A less perfect quality is called an aptitude. To these correspond, in natural things, the act in the one case and the power in the other.

V. What jurists call a faculty we shall henceforth call a Right, properly or strictly so called; and in this term are included: (a) Power, when used over oneself, which is called liberty; (b) Authority, when power is used over others, as in the exercise of paternal or a master's rights; (c) Ownership or Property, either full, or, such as usufruct or pledge, less full; and (d) Credit, where one is entitled to a debt due from another.

VI. But, again, this faculty is double. It is either Private, when understood of a particular use, or Public—and superior to a private right—when exercised by a community over persons and things for the common good. Thus, the regal power has beneath it both the paternal and the master's right; and so, in relation to the property of individuals, is the dominion of the King for the common good greater than that of the individuals themselves. Thus every citizen is under a greater obligation in relation to the public demands of the State than to the demands of his creditor.

VII. An aptitude is what Aristotle calls a moral desert or claim. . . .

VIII. (1) That is Expletory Justice, properly and strictly named justice, which has regard to faculty; and Aristotle terms such justice contractual. This term is too restricted, however, for it is not by force of any contract that he who detains my property should restore it to me, and yet that obligation of his comes within this class of justice. Wherefore Aristotle refers to it elsewhere, more happily, as Corrective Justice. Attributive Justice, called by Aristotle Distributive Justice, is that justice which has regard to aptitude. It is the companion of those virtues which are beneficial to others, such as generosity, mercy, and prudence in government. (2) According to Aristotle, Expletory Justice proceeds by simple proportion, and Attributive Justice by comparison—which latter is alone termed proportion by mathematicians. This distinction, however, though often true, is not so always. Nor, indeed, does Expletory Justice differ *per se* from Attributive in such a manner, but they differ, rather, as we have just pointed out, in their respective subject-matters. So, in a contract of partnership, the division is made according to a proportion of comparison. And if only one man is found to be fit for a public office Attributive Justice may confer it upon him by nothing else than simple reckoning. (3) Nor is it truer what is said by some—that common property is the subject of Attributive Justice and private property that of Expletory Justice. On the contrary, if anyone is about to dispose of his property by will it is to Attributive Justice that he usually has regard. And the State is no less bound by the obligation of Expletory Justice when it refunds from the common stock what private citizens have spent on public affairs. And this distinction was correctly learnt by Cyrus from his tutor, as would appear when Cyrus awarded the smaller coat to the younger boy and the greater to the older. . . .

IX. (1) Then there is a third signification of Right—that of Law, in the widest sense of the word, which is a rule of moral

acts obliging to what is right. " Obliging " is necessary, for
advice and mere precepts, honoured, it may be, but not obliging,
do not come within the idea of Law or Right in this sense.
Permission is not properly an act of law but rather an inaction,
except so far as it obliges another to raise no impediment to him
to whom permission is given. But, as we have said, the obliging
is to the right, not merely to the just, because the right in this
sense belongs not only to the matter of justice alone, as we
have already explained, but also to that of the other virtues.
Still, what is right, as being barely just, may be loosely said to
be just. (2) The most acceptable division of Right in this general
sense is that of Aristotle. On the one hand, there is Natural Law,
and, on the other, Voluntary Law, or, as he calls it, " Legal
Law," or Positive Law, the word " law " being taken in its
stricter sense. The Hebrews have the same division. . . .

X. (1) Natural Law is the dictate of right reason. It indicates
whether an act is morally right or wrong, according as it complies
or disagrees with rational nature itself. Such an act is consequently either prescribed or forbidden, as the case may be, by
God the Author of Nature. (2) Acts about which there is such a
dictate are either obligatory or unlawful *per se*, and so are to be
understood as being necessarily prescribed or forbidden by God
Himself; and this makes Natural Law differ not only from
Human Law but also from Voluntary Divine Law, inasmuch as
the latter does not prescribe or forbid those things which are
obligatory or unlawful *per se* and by their own nature, but by
forbidding them renders them unlawful and by prescribing them
renders them obligatory. (3) But in order to obtain a just idea
of Natural Law it must be noted that there are certain things
said to belong to that law which do not belong to it properly, but,
as the schoolmen love to say, reductively or indirectly. By this
is meant that Natural Law is not opposed to them, just as—to
repeat what we have said—some things are called just which have
no injustice in them. Yet sometimes, by an abuse of the term,
there are certain things which reason regards as decent, or as
comparatively good, which, though not matters of obligation, are
usually said to belong to Natural Law. (4) It must be known,
moreover, that the Natural Law deals not only with things which
exist independently of the human will, but also with many things

which are the consequence of some act of that will. So property, as it now exists, was introduced by human will. But once it is introduced, Natural Law itself indicates that it is wrong for me to take from you, against your will, that which is yours. . . . (5) And, besides, Natural Law is so immutable that even God Himself cannot change it. For though the power of God be boundless, yet it may be said that there are some things to which it does not extend. Indeed, when we speak of these things so, it is only in a manner of speaking which, so far from expressing anything at all, involves a manifest contradiction. Therefore, as it is impossible even for God so to make it that twice two are not four, so He cannot make that which is intrinsically bad not to be bad; and this is what Aristotle means when he says that of some things the name alone involves the idea of vice and depravity. For as the being of things, when and how they exist, does not depend on anything else, so with the properties necessarily involved in that being. Such is the evil of some actions when compared with a nature guided by right reason. And so even God suffers Himself to be judged according to this rule, as may be seen in Genesis, xviii. 25, &c. (6) Yet sometimes it happens that in these acts which Natural Law prescribes or forbids some show of change may mislead the superficial observer, Natural Law not in fact having changed, but only the subject-matter of the law. For instance, if my creditor give me a receipt for what I owe him, I am not then bound to pay him; not because Natural Law has ceased to require me to pay what I owe but because what I owe ceases to be a debt. . . . So if God should order someone to be slain, or his goods to be taken, murder or theft— words which involve the idea of vice—are not thereby made lawful. But that will not be murder or theft which is done by the express command of the Supreme Lord of life and property. (7) And there are certain things which accord with Natural Law, not absolutely, but according to circumstances. So community of property was a natural condition until private ownership had been introduced; and so also, before laws had been made, a man's assertion of his right by his own might.

XI. (1) But in the Roman law-books two classes of this immutable law are distinguished. There is that which is common to both men and animals, which they term, in the stricter sense,

Natural Law; and there is that which is peculiar to mankind, and which they often style the Law of Nations. This distinction, however, is of little or no practical use, for no creature is properly susceptible of law unless of a nature which can observe general precepts. . . . [So] we do not admit that there can be any idea of law in horses and lions. . . . (2) If at any time that idea be attributed to brutes, it is improperly so done, and only because some mere shadow or trace of reason is to be found in them. Indeed, it is quite immaterial to the problem of the actual nature of law whether a particular action, the subject of Natural Law, such as the upbringing of offspring, is common to us with other living creatures, or is one, such as the worship of God, that is peculiar to us only.

XII. (1) That anything is or is not of Natural Law is usually proved by arguments either *a priori* or *a posteriori*, the latter mode of proof being the more popular and the former the more subtle. It is proof *a priori* when there is shown the necessary agreement or disagreement with a rational and social nature of the thing in question. It is proof *a posteriori* if, without absolute certainty but yet with greatest probability, that is regarded as of the Natural Law which is so believed to be by all, or, at least, the more civilised peoples. And inasmuch as a universal effect requires a universal cause, no other cause can well be assigned for this general opinion than that general sense which is called common. . . .

XIII. The other kind of law, we told you, is Voluntary [Positive] Law, which has its origin in the will. And this is either Human or Divine.

XIV. (1) Let us begin with the human, because that is the more widely known. This is either Civil Law [national or municipal law] or law in a more restricted or in a wider sense. Civil Law is so called because it proceeds from the civil power; and it is that power which governs the State, which, in its turn, is a perfect union of free men associated for protection by law and for their common benefit. Law is a more restricted sense, not proceeding from the civil power itself, though subject to it, is various, including paternal precepts, a master's commands, and the like. But law in the wider sense is the Law of Nations, being that which derives its obliging power from the will of all nations, or, at least, of many. We have said " of many," because scarcely any law is to be found common to all peoples outside Natural Law, which itself is usually also called the Law of Nations. Rather, what is often the Law of Nations in one part of the world is not so in another, as we shall explain later on in connection with capture and *postliminium*. (2) And the Law of Nations is proved in the same manner as the unwritten Civil Law, namely, by long usage and the testimony of its professors; for this law, as Dio Chrysostom says, is " the invention of time and experience," and here the great historians are of the greatest service to us.

XV. (1) What, now, is Voluntary Divine Law? We know quite well from the name itself. We know this at least—that it has its origin in the Divine will; and so it may be distinguished from Natural Law, which also, as we have already said, can in some sense be called Divine. And we here recall what Anaxarchus said, though too generally : " God does not will a thing because it is just; but it is just, that is legally obligatory, because He wills it." (2) This law was given either to all mankind or to one people only. And we find that it was given by God to all mankind on three occasions—the first, immediately after the creation of man; the second, upon the reinstatement of mankind after the Flood; and the third, on man's more sublime reinstatement through Christ. Without doubt these three laws oblige all men, as and when they acquire a sufficient knowledge of them.

XVI. (1—8) To only one people, the Hebrews, did God specially give laws, . . . the Mosaic Law, which binds only those to whom it was given, and not strangers. . . . Hence we may conclude that we are bound by no part of that law. . . .

XVII. (1) Since, therefore, the Mosaic Law cannot, as we have just shown, impose any direct obligation upon us, let us see if it can have any other use—first, in this matter of the laws of war, and, next, in other like questions. This is important in regard to many matters. (2) First, then, the Mosaic Law shows that its commands are not contrary to Natural Law. And because that law is eternal and immutable, as we have already said, it is impossible that God, Who is never unjust, should command anything contrary to it. Add to this that the Mosaic Law is called pure and right in several places in the Scriptures. . . .

CHAPTER II.—WHETHER WAR CAN EVER BE JUST.

Having seen what are the sources of law, let us now come to the first and most general question, which is this : Can any war be just, or, in other words, is war ever lawful?

I. (1) But this question itself, as well as others which follow, must be first examined by reference to Natural Law. Cicero learnedly proves, in *De Finibus* and elsewhere, from the writings of the Stoics, that there are not only certain first principles of nature, but also, of higher value than these, there are certain other principles which are their consequences. He calls such a first principle that instinct which is born in and is common to all animals, by which each desires his own preservation and is impelled, on the one hand, to love his own well-being and to do all he can to maintain it, and, on the other, to avoid destruction and all that may tend to it. So there is no one who does not prefer to have all his limbs whole and fit rather than·maimed and distorted. It is man's first duty to preserve himself in the state of nature, his next being to retain what is in conformity with nature and reject all that is opposed to it. (2) These things being premised, there follows the knowledge of how to conform our actions to reason rather than to the body. And this conformity, which involves the idea of the reasonable [*honestum*], must be regarded as far preferable to any merely bodily satisfaction, for the first principles of nature commend us to right reason as something which should be much dearer to us than those things by which we are brought to it. These things are absolutely true, and easily allowed, without further proof, by all men of sound judgment. So, in examining Natural Law we must first discover what agrees with the first principles of nature, and then we must proceed to that which, though of later origin, is yet more excellent and is not so much merely to be accepted when it presents itself as actually to be sought by every means. (3) But that which we call reasonable is more or less determined by circumstances. At one moment it rests upon a point, so to speak, so that he who departs from it only to the least degree falls straight into evil. At another it stands upon a broader foundation, so that while he who respects it acts commendably, yet he may, without doing anything dishonourable, act at variance with it or even quite indifferently to it, determined, in his action, by the presence or absence of certain conditions. Between opposites of another class, such as black and white, something intermediate is found, either a tint approximating towards one or the other or a tint absolutely neutral. And it is in relation to this latter class of cases that we find laws, both divine and human, rendering that obligatory which in itself is only commendable. But, as we have already said, that which is to be discovered when Natural Law is in question, is whether a particular thing can be done without injustice. And what is necessarily repugnant to a rational and social nature is to be regarded as unjust. (4) There is nothing in the first principles of nature that is repugnant to war. On the contrary, everything rather favours it. For the object of war, which is the preservation of life and limb, and the retention or acquisition of things useful to life, is very agreeable to those first principles. And so, if to attain this object it is necessary to use force, those principles will offer no opposition, for nature has given strength to every living creature in order to defend and help itself. . . . (5) But right reason and the nature of society, which must be examined in the next and chief place, do not prohibit all force, but only that which is repugnant to society, namely, that which invades the right of another. For society, by its general strength and agreement, assures to each the safe possession of that which is his own. And this can easily be understood to be the case at a stage of social development in which what we now call private property had not come into existence, for even then a man's life, limb and liberty would so peculiarly belong to him that they could not be attacked by another without his suffering a distinct wrong. So also, to have used things that were then in common, and to have appropriated as much of them as nature required, would have been the right of a possessor, and he who would have invaded that right would have done the possessor a wrong. This, however, is now much more easily understood since private property has taken shape either by law, or custom. . . . (6) It is therefore not against the nature of society to provide for, and to take care of, one's self, provided the right of another is not infringed. And so that force which does not violate another's right is not unjust . . .

II. (1) What we have just said, that all war is not repugnant to Natural Law, may be further proved from sacred history. Thus, when Abraham, with his armed servants and allies, had vanquished the four kings who had plundered Sodom, God, through His priest Melchisedec, approved that deed. . . . Yet, as the story goes, Abraham had taken up arms without the special mandate of God. And so, Abraham being not only a very holy man but also a very wise one, as we learn even from the heathens Berosius and Orpheus, it must be taken that he acted as he did under warrant of Natural Law. . . . (2) Moreover, God prescribed for His people general and permanent rules of waging war, and so made manifest that even without His special warrant a just war is possible . . . And since nothing is there declared as to what are just causes of war it is implied that these are easily discoverable by the light of nature. . . .

III. (1) Our doctrine may also be proved by the consent of all nations, and particularly of judicious men. Cicero, speaking of force in the defence of our lives, adduces Nature herself as a witness. . . . (2) And this has so manifest an equity, that even in beasts whose laws, as I have already said, are no more than shadows, we can distinguish between force which assaults and that which only defends. . . .

IV. (1) Therefore, it is quite clear that by Natural Law, which may also be called the Law of Nations, all warfare is not to be condemned. (2) And history and the laws and customs of all peoples teach us quite plainly that war is not condemned by the voluntary Law of Nations. On the contrary, according to Hermogenianus, war was introduced by the Law of Nations. This statement, however, should, in my opinion, be understood in a slightly different sense to that in which it is popularly received. Rather, a certain mode of warfare was introduced by the Law of Nations, so that wars that conform to that mode have, by the rules of war, certain well-defined incidents. Whence arises a distinction, of which we shall presently make use, between " solemn " wars, also called just or full or complete wars, and " non-solemn " wars which yet, on that account, do not cease to be just, that is, to conform to law and justice. For, as will hereafter appear, the Law of Nations neither allows nor condemns " non-solemn " or informal wars, provided the cause be just. By the Law of Nations, says Livy, it is allowed to repel arms by arms. And Florentinus declares it to be in accordance with the Law of Nations to repel violence and wrong in defence of our lives.

V. (1) Concerning Instituted Divine Law the difficulty is greater. But let none here object that Natural Law is immutable, and that consequently nothing contrary to it can be prescribed by God. This is indeed true of what Natural Law actually forbids or prescribes, but not of what that law only permits, for things of the latter kind, not properly being subject to Natural Law but extraneous to it, may be either forbidden or prescribed. (2) The first objection usually brought against war by some is that of the law which was given to Noah and his posterity . . . . but the forbidding of the shedding of blood is of no wider extent than the law " Thou shalt not kill," which, it is obvious, prohibits neither capital punishment nor lawful war . . . . (6) And we have, for this view, the great authority of Abraham, who, not being ignorant of the law given to Noah, took up arms against the four kings, believing, in fact, that his action was not repugnant to that law. So Moses commanded his people to fight against the Amalekites, who had attacked them, and in doing this he followed, apparently, Natural Law, for he does not seem to have particularly consulted God about this matter. Moreover, capital punishment was not inflicted upon murderers only, but also on other heinous offenders, and that by God's chosen people as well as by other nations.

VI. (1) The arguments against war which are taken out of the Gospel are more plausible. But in examining these I shall not assume, as many do, that there is nothing in the Gospel, besides points of faith and the sacraments, which is not enjoined by Natural Law. That, in the commonly received sense, is not, I think, true. (2) I willingly grant that nothing is commanded us in the Gospel that is not naturally reasonable; but I see no ground to hold that we are bound to nothing more by the laws of Christ than by those of Nature. . . . (3) Nor shall I follow those who presume to say that Christ, when delivering the precepts in Matthew v. *et seq.*, was only interpreting the Mosaic Law . . . .

VII. (1) Omitting, then, the arguments of less weight, we have, as first and chief testimony that the right of waging war is not absolutely taken away by the law of Christ, those words of Paul in Timothy ii., 1, 2, 3 [as developed in] Romans xiii., 4 . . . . (3) Where we also find a second argument. . . . (5) The third argument is taken from the words of John the Baptist, when asked by the Jewish soldiers (of whom many thousands were in the Roman army, as appears from Josephus and other writers)—What shall we do to flee from the wrath of God? He did not bid them to leave the army, which he ought to have done if such had been God's will, but answered only that they should abstain from extortion and fraud and be content with their wages. But to these words of the Baptist, which clearly approve of a military life, many answer that his exhortations and Christ's precepts differ so widely that he seemed to preach one doctrine, and Christ another. This, however, I cannot admit, for both John and our Saviour sum up their doctrine in the same terms, namely, Repent, for the Kingdom of Heaven is at hand. . . . (6) The fourth argument is one which appears to me to have no small weight. If the right of inflicting capital punishment and of defending citizens from thieves and robbers with the sword be taken away there would immediately follow the greatest license of crime and a deluge, as it were, of evils, since even now crime is scarcely repressed by the judicial power. So, if it had been in the mind of Christ to introduce such a state of things as was never heard of, He would certainly have declared it in the clearest and most certain words. . . . (7) My fifth point is that it cannot be shewn by any argument that the judicial law of Moses was abolished before Jerusalem should be destroyed and with it all existence and hope of a Jewish State. For neither is any term fixed by that law itself, nor did Christ or the Apostles say anything as to its abrogation, unless so far as that may seem to be involved, as I have already said, in the destruction of the State. On the contrary . . . Christ Himself, in the preface to His commandments, declares that He has not come to destroy the law but to fulfil it . . . (9) My sixth argument is from the case of Cornelius the centurion, who received from Christ the Holy Spirit, the undoubted sign of justification, and, moreover, was baptized in the name of Christ by the Apostle Peter. Yet we do not find that he resigned his commission or was advised by Peter so to do. . . . (10) **A** seventh and similar argument may be gathered from the conversion of Sergius Paulus (whom I lately mentioned); for in its story there is no suggestion of his quitting the magistracy or of any admonition that he should do so. (11) The eighth argument is from the Apostle Paul, who, hearing that the Jews lay in wait for him, desired that the fact should be made known to the tribune. And when the tribune furnished him with soldiers, whose convoy would ensure his safety from any attack, he made no objection whatever. Nor did he tell the tribune or the soldiers that it was displeasing to God to repel force by force. And yet this is that same Paul who never neglected an opportunity to teach men their duty, and whose one wish was that no one else should be guilty of that neglect. (12) Ninthly. That which is a natural end of a good and right act cannot itself be other than good and right. It is right that we pay taxes; this, as Paul expresses it, being a precept binding upon the conscience. Yet one object of the taxes is that our governors may have the means to protect the good and coerce the evil. . . . (13) A tenth argument is found in Acts xxv., 11, where Paul says, " If I be an offender, or have committed any thing worthy of death, I refuse not to die. . . ."

Having proved that capital punishment may be rightly inflicted after the coming of Christ, I consider that it is also proved that certain warfare may be rightly carried on, that is, waged against a company of armed evildoers who must be overcome in battle before they will admit their guilt. For though the power and resistance of the evildoers are matter for consideration in prudent deliberation, yet they have no relation to the question of who or what is right. (14) The eleventh argument is that in the Revelations some wars of the righteous are predicted with manifest approbation. (15) That the law of Christ abolishes the law of Moses only so far as it separates the Hebrews from the other peoples, is my twelfth argument. Such things as are accounted right by nature, and by the general consent of civilised peoples, it was so far from taking away, that it comprehends them under the general precept of all honesty and virtue. Now the punishment of crimes, and the repelling of injuries by arms, are regarded as naturally laudable, and are classed under the virtues of justice and beneficence. . . .

VIII. Let us now also see what arguments are brought in
support of the opposite opinion, so that the pious reader may more
easily decide which are the more weighty.   (1) First usually
brought up is the prophecy of Isaiah, that the nations would beat
their swords into ploughshares and their spears into pruning-hooks,
and would no more take up the sword one against the other and no
longer learn war.   But this prophecy must be understood either
conditionally, as many others are, or unconditionally. If conditionally, then it is subject to the existence of an international society
in which all nations have submitted to the law of Christ and
actually carry it out.   Under such circumstances there would be
nothing wanting to fulfilment on the part of God, for it is certain
that, if all were Christians and lived as Christians, there would
be no wars. . . .   If unconditionally, then it is obvious that the
prophecy has not yet been fulfilled, that fulfilment and the conversion of the Jews being as yet only a matter of expectation.
But take the prophecy which way you will, conditional or uncon-
ditional, nothing can be inferred therefrom against the lawfulness
of war so long as there are people who will not allow lovers of
peace to enjoy peace, but, rather, assail them with violence . . . .
(2) Many arguments are usually taken from the fifth chapter of
Matthew, and in order to judge their value it is necessary to
remember what was said a little before : That if Christ had proposed
to abolish all capital punishment and the right of war He would
have done so in the most plain and specific terms on account of
the great importance and the novelty of the proposal, and the more
so because no Jew could believe otherwise than that the laws of
Moses concerning judicial affairs of the State were absolutely
obligatory upon the Jews so long as that State should exist.
Bearing this in mind let us proceed to consider in order the force
of each passage.   (3) The second argument, then, in favour of our
opponents' views is to be sought in these words: " Ye have heard
that it hath been said, An eye for an eye, and a tooth for a tooth :
But I say unto you, That ye resist not the evil man: but
whosoever shall smite thee on thy right cheek, turn to him
the other also."   Hence some infer that no injury ought to be
resisted or satisfaction secured therefor, either publicly or privately.
Yet the words themselves do not say this, for Christ is not here
speaking to magistrates, but to those who are injured.   Nor does

he speak of all injuries, but only of slight ones such as a box on
the ear, for the last words restrict the generality of those preceding.
(4) So in the following precept: " If any man will sue thee at
law, and take away thy coat, let him have thy cloke also." It
is not every appeal to a judge or umpire that is here prohibited,
according to Paul, who does not forbid all litigation (1 Cor. vi., 4),
but only that of Christians before heathen tribunals. And herein
he holds up to the Christians the example of the Jews, among
whom the saying was current, that " He who brings the cause
of an Israelite before strangers, profanes the name of God . . .'."
(5) So in what follows: " If any man shall compel thee to go
with him one mile, go with him twain." Our Lord did not say
a hundred miles, which distance might take a man too far away
from his business, but one, and, if need be, two, which is no
more than a trifling walk. The meaning then is this, that in
matters of small moment we are not to insist too much upon our
rights, but rather yield more than is demanded, so that our
patience and kindness may become known to all. (6) And then
follows: " Give to him that asketh thee, and from him that would
borrow of thee turn not thou away." If you understand this
without any sort of limitation, nothing could be harder. He who
takes not care of his own family is worse than an infidel, says
Paul (1 Tim. v., 8). Let us then follow Paul, the best interpreter
of his Master's law (2 Cor. iii., 13). . . . (8) In such circumstances [tolerable injuries], Christ enjoins patience. . . . (9) The
third argument is usually taken from the following passage from
St. Matthew: " Ye have heard that it hath been said, Thou shalt
love thy neighbour, and hate thine enemy; but I say unto you,
Love your enemies, bless them that curse you, do good to them
that hate you, and pray for them that despitefully use you, and
persecute you." For there are those who consider that both
capital punishment and war are repugnant to such love and good
feeling for one's enemies, but this is easily answered if we have
regard to the actual words of the Hebrew law. The Hebrews
were commanded to love their neighbour, that is, a Hebrew. . . .
But none the less, the magistrates were commanded to put
murderers and other heinous offenders to death; the eleven tribes
justly made war upon the tribe of Benjamin for a horrid crime
(Judg. xx.), and David, who fought the battles of the Lord,

rightly recovered by arms from Ishbosheth the kingdom promised to him. (12) The fourth objection is taken from Rom. xii., 17: " Recompense no man evil for evil, &c." But here also the same answer as before is obvious, for at the very time that God said, " Vengeance is mine, I will repay," capital punishment was inflicted and the laws of war were already written. . . . (13) . . . Paul says that the public authorities are the ministers of God, and avengers to execute wrath, that is, punishment, against evildoers; and so he most plainly distinguishes between punishment for the sake of the public good, inflicted by the minister of God and referable to the vengeance reserved by God, and that private and particular revenge which he had prohibited just before. For if you include in this prohibition that punishment for the sake of the public good, what could be more absurd than, when he had bid them abstain from capital punishment, he should immediately add that public authorities were ordained by God to this end, to inflict punishment in His stead? . . . (17) But what was said to Peter, that " He that smiteth with the sword shall perish by the sword," since it does not refer to war in the ordinary sense of the word, but properly to private battle—for Christ Himself gives as a reason for prohibiting or neglecting His own defence that His kingdom was not of this world—will be more properly discussed in its own place.

IX. (1) Whenever there is any doubt as to the sense of any writing, it is usual to attach great weight both to subsequent usage and to the authority of the learned, and especially should this be so in the case of the Holy Scriptures, for it is not probable that the Churches which were founded by the Apostles should either suddenly, or universally, have fallen away from what the Apostles had briefly prescribed in writing, or, more fully, verbally explained to them, or even reduced into practice. Still, as those who argue against war are accustomed to allege some sayings of the early Christians, I will make three remarks as to this. (2) My first point is that nothing can be adduced from these sayings which is any more than the private opinion of individuals as distinguished from the official view of the Churches. Moreover, those whose sayings are quoted are mostly men who loved to follow a path of their own and teach something striking. Of such are Origen and Tertullian—writers who are not even consistent with themselves. . . . (3) My second observation is that Christians often disparaged or avoided the military life because of the conditions of the age, which scarcely permitted the military life without the practice of some acts repugnant to the Christian law. . . . (4) My third remark is that the primitive Christians were consumed with so ardent a desire for perfection, that often what was only Divine counsel would be taken for Divine command. . . . Thus Lactantius says that a just man, such as he would have a Christian to be, will not make war; but he also says that he should not go to sea. And how many primitive Christians inveighed against second marriages? . . .

X. (1) But now to establish our case. First, we are not without authors, and the more ancient too, who maintain that Christians may lawfully inflict capital punishment and—which follows— engage in war. Clemens Alexandrinus, for example . . . . (2) But setting aside individuals let us come to what should have greatest weight, the official pronouncements of the Church. I say, then, that never were any soldiers as such refused baptism, or excommunicated, which ought to have been the case, and would have been, if the military life had been inconsistent with the conditions of the new covenant. As to which reference may be made to the Constitutions of Clemens . . . . Tertullian, too, told the emperor Marcus Aurelius that rain had been sent in answer to the prayers of the Christian soldiers. And in the *De Corona* he says that the soldier who had thrown away the garland was braver than his comrades, and reminds the emperor that he had many Christian soldiers. (3) Add to this that some soldiers who suffered torments and death for Christ's sake received from the Church the same honour as other martyrs, amongst them being noted three companions of St. Paul. (4) That the Christians of those days did not care to be present at capital punishments is not to be wondered at, since they were themselves so often the victims of such punishments. . . . (5) [And among the bishops, St. Ambrose says] . . . " To go to war is no fault, but to do it purely for plunder is a sin . . . ." (11) But in support of our view we have the express judgment of the Church in the first Council of Arles, held under Constantine; for its Third Canon declares that those who throw away their arms in time of peace are to be excluded from communion, that is, those who desert from the army at a time when there is no persecution. For the Christians so meant the word " peace " to be understood, as appears from Cyprian and others. And let us add the example of the soldiers under Julian, Christians of no little piety, who were ready by their death to give testimony to Christ, and of whom St. Ambrose speaks . . . . And so, long before, the Theban legion under Diocletian, who were converted to Christianity. . . . (12) Let it suffice here to quote their words— addressed to the emperor—which, with impressive brevity, express the duty of the Christian soldier: "We offer our hands against any enemy whatsoever, though we hold it a crime to stain them with the blood of the innocent. Our right hands know how to fight against the wicked and the enemy, but not how to butcher the good man and our fellow citizen. We remember that we first took up arms for our fellow citizens, rather than against them. We have always fought for justice, the good, and the safety of the innocent, and these have hitherto been the rewards of our courage. We have fought for our faith, and how shall we keep our allegiance to you if we do not keep it to our God? . . . "

BOOK II.

CHAPTER I.—OF THE CAUSES OF WAR; AND FIRST, OF SELF-DEFENCE AND THE DEFENCE OF OUR PROPERTY.

I. (1) Let us come to the causes of wars. And by causes I mean "just" causes; for there are other causes which are merely considerations of utility, and are therefore quite distinct from those in which the sense of right, or the " just," operates. . . . (3) Just cause is no less requisite in public wars than in private. Hence Seneca asks how the homicide of individuals is a crime while the slaughter of peoples is a glory. For, though public wars, being undertaken by public authority, have certain juridical results, as have judicial sentences—of which hereafter—yet they are not thereby the less criminal if begun without just reason. . . . And the query of St. Augustine is much to the point: " Without justice what are empires but so many great robberies? . . . (4) A just cause of war can be nothing else than an injury received. . . .

II. (1) Now, clearly, there are as many causes of war as there are of actions at law. . . . (2) Most writers assign three just causes of war—defence, recovery of property, and punishment. . . (3) . . . The first cause, therefore, of a just war is an injury which, though not yet done, threatens either our person or property.

III. We have already said that if a man is menaced by a present force so that his life is in inevitable danger, then he may not only attack but even destroy his aggressor; and from this premise, which all must allow, we have proved that private war may, in some cases, be lawful. And it must be noted that this right of self-defence is inherent and fundamental and depends

not at all upon the injustice or wrong-doing of the aggressor. So,
I do not lose my right of self-defence even if he has no intention
to do wrong, as when, for instance, he is performing his duty as
a soldier, or mistakes me for someone else, or acts as one insane
or in a dream—all of which we have read of.   It is sufficient that
I am not bound to suffer the wrong he threatens any more than
any injury with which I might be threatened by a wild beast.

IV. (1) It is a disputed question, however, whether we may
kill or trample down innocent persons who, interposing, hinder
a defence or escape by which alone we can avoid death.   There
are some, even divines, who think it lawful. . . .

V. (1) It is necessary that the danger should be present, and,
as it were, immediate.   But I have no doubt that if a man is
actually taking up weapons, obviously with the intent to kill
another, the latter may anticipate and prevent his intention;
and this is so because in the moral code, as in the laws of nature,
there is no rule which does not admit of some latitude in application. Yet they are greatly in error, and deceive others, who presume
that a bare apprehension of danger would justify a precautionary
homicide. . . . (2) . . . If a danger can be otherwise avoided, or
if it is not quite certain that it cannot be otherwise avoided, delay
gives opportunity for many remedies and many chances, or, as
the ancient saw has it, many things may intervene between the
mouth and the morsel.   Nor are there wanting divines and jurists
who extend this indulgence even farther.

XI. We now come to those injuries that affect our property.
And here, if we have regard to corrective justice, I shall not deny
that it is lawful to slay a robber if it be necessary for the preservation of our goods. . . .

XIII. (1) . . . [But according to the Gospel] if our property
can be preserved without running the risk of slaying a man, that
is all right.   But if not, then the property is better lost, unless
it is something upon which our life and that of our family depend
and which cannot be recovered at law. . . .

XIV. . . . The law, though, neither gives nor ought to give to
any man the right privately to kill anyone, not even those who
deserve death, except for the most atrocious crimes, for otherwise
there would be no need for courts of justice.   Therefore, when the
law allows a thief to be killed with impunity it must be under-

stood only as dispensing from punishment and not as conferring a right.

XVI. What we have so far said of the right of defending one's person and one's property belongs properly to private war, but, subject to difference of circumstances, it is also applicable to public war. In private war the right of defence is, as it were, a momentary and temporary one, disappearing as soon as the tribunal is available for the settlement of the matter in dispute. But in public war, since it arises only because there is no such tribunal or that tribunal has ceased to function, that right has permanency and continually develops with the occurrence of new wrongs and injuries. Moreover, in private war the right is limited to mere defence, while public authorities exact satisfaction as well. Hence, a danger which is not present but threatens from afar may be warded off by such authorities, though not directly (for, as we have above shown, that would be unjust), but indirectly, that is to say, by exacting satisfaction for a wrong already begun, but not completed—with which we shall deal elsewhere.

XVII. But I can hardly approve the doctrine of some writers, that by the Law of Nations we may rightly take up arms to enfeeble a rising power which, if too much augmented, may become dangerous to us. Undoubtedly, in arriving at a decision about a proposed war, these things may be taken into calculation, though not as a matter of justice but as a matter of interest, so that, if the war be just on other grounds it may, on this account, be prudent to declare it. And not any of the authorities cited say anything else. But it is a doctrine contrary to every principle of equity that justice allows us to resort to force in order to injure another merely because there is a possibility that he may injure us. Indeed, human life is such that we can never enjoy a condition of complete security. Against uncertain fears protection must be sought in divine providence and innocent precaution, and not in the exercise of our strength.

XVIII. (1) No less unsatisfactory is that doctrine, based upon the assumption that only a few are content to proportion their vengeance to the injury received, that a defence by those who have brought upon themselves a just war is right. For that fear of an uncertainty cannot give a right to take up arms. And so an accused person has no right, because he fears he may not be fairly punished, forcibly to resist arrest by the ministers of justice. (2) But he who has wronged another ought first to offer to the latter a satisfaction at the arbitration of a good man, and then, if that offer be refused, his defence will be just.

CHAPTER XXII.—OF UNJUST CAUSES OF WAR.

I. (1) When we were speaking of the causes of war we divided them into two classes—namely, justificatory, or justifying causes, and suasory causes, or motives. . . .

II. But there are some who engage in war for neither of these causes, being, as Tacitus says, greedy of danger for its own sake. And so inhuman is such action that Aristotle calls it brutishness. . . .

III. (1) Still, most of those who wage war, while they all have suasory causes, or motives, yet only in some cases have justificatory causes, having none in other cases. And to those who thus fight frankly without justification we may follow the Roman jurisconsults and apply the term robbers—men whose right to possess a thing being challenged can assert no other than that of mere possession. . . . (2) Of this stamp was Brennus, who said that everything belonged to him who was the stronger. . . .

IV. Some there are who engage in war for only apparently justifying causes, which, when brought to the bar of right reason, are found to be unjust; and, as Livy says, there does not then appear to be any struggle for the right, but rather a ruthless aggression of the mighty. Most kings, says Plutarch, use these two names of war and peace only as pieces of money, to obtain, not justice, but what they want. But though unjust causes may be recognised fairly well by reference to the just causes already mentioned, inasmuch as the straight line is the indicator of the crooked, still we shall specially note the principal instances of the unjust in order to make matters as plain as possible.

V. (1) Mere dread of a neighbouring Power is not, as we have already said, a sufficient cause. For a defensive war to be just, it ought to be necessary, which is not the case unless it is clear that our neighbour has not only the power, but the intention, to injure us, and unless the evidence of that intention is practically conclusive. (2) So we cannot very well assent to the opinion of those who consider that a just cause of war arises where a neighbouring Power, not being precluded by treaty from so doing, erects in its own territory a castle or some other fortified place which may at some time or other prove dangerous to us. For such possible dangers should be met by erecting like places within our own territories, and taking like precautions, rather than having recourse to war. . . .

VI. Nor do the advantages which may accrue to us from war create a right comparable to that which is derived from necessity.

VIII. Nor is there any more justice in the desire to migrate from one place to another in order to occupy a more fruitful land in the stead of swamp and desert, as, according to Tacitus, was the cause of most of the wars among the ancient Germans.

IX. And equally unjust is it, under pretext of discovery, to raid occupied territory, even though the occupants are godless and almost brainless savages.

X. (1) Ownership, including that of such occupants, involves neither moral virtue, religious faith, nor perfect intellect, though it seems that this may be fairly argued—that if there should be any people entirely destitute of reason their ownership is limited to such things as, by charity, are necessary for the preservation of their life. What we have already said as to the rules of the Natural Law of Nations for the preservation of the property of infants and persons of unsound mind is to be applied to those peoples with whom agreements can be made; and if—which is very doubtful—there be any peoples entirely without reason, they are not of that class. (2) . . . But it is another question how far ownership may be lost because of grave offences and opposition to nature or human society, and with this we deal when we come to consider the right to punish.

XI. Another unjust cause of war is the desire for liberty, whether that of individuals or that—autonomy or self-government —of States, as if it were a natural and constant right of every man or State. For when liberty is claimed as the natural heritage of men and peoples it must be understood only as a natural right as it existed before any human action in derogation of it, and as an exemption from slavery, but not an absolute incompatibility with slavery. So, though a man is not a slave by nature, yet there is no natural right which prevents him ever being a slave. For in the latter sense no one is free. " No one is born either freeman or slave," says Albutius, " but fortune gives these names to them afterwards." . . .

XII. Nor is it less unjust to seek to subjugate, by force of arms, those we deem fit only to be slaves, who, as the philosophers sometimes say, are slaves by nature, for we have no right to force a man even to what is to his advantage. For those who have the enjoyment of their reason ought, unless another has a right over them, to have a free choice of what may seem to their advantage or otherwise. . . .

XVI. It must also be understood that if a man owes anything to another, not in strictness of law, but by some other virtue, as, for instance, generosity, gratitude, pity, or charity, then as that cannot be exacted in a court of justice so it cannot be requisitioned by force of arms. For either of these remedies presumes something more than a moral obligation, and that the obligee has a strictly legal right such as is sometimes involved by both Divine and human laws in obligations created by virtues other than that of justice; and when this occurs there is introduced into the obligation a new element which brings the obligation into relation with the idea of justice, and where that element is absent a war to enforce the so-called obligation is waged for an unjust cause. . . .

XVII. (1) We must observe, too, that it often happens that there may actually be a just cause for a war, and yet the giving effect to it may become wrong from the intention of the agent, as when some motive, not unlawful in itself, more powerfully incites him than the right he purports to assert. Such a motive might be, for instance, the vindication of outraged honour, or the acquisition of some advantage, private or public, which is expected to accrue from the war, the motive being considered independently of the justifying cause of the war; or the motive may be clearly unlawful, as where pleasure is to be found in another's misfortune without regard to any good. . .

CHAPTER XXIII.—OF DOUBTFUL CAUSES OF WAR.

I. Very true is it, as Aristotle wrote, that there is not the same degree of certainty in moral science as there is in mathematics. . . . So, between that which ought to be done and that which is prohibited there is a permissible mean, which, however, tending, as it does, now towards the one extreme and now towards the other, is often of doubtful character, like twilight or lukewarm water. . . .

II. (2) It often happens, too, that our judgment does not reach decision, but hesitates, doubtful. Then if that hesitation cannot be determined by careful consideration, we must follow the rule of Cicero—"Do nothing the justice of which we question," is its substance. Or, as the Hebrew Rabbis say, "Abstain from what is doubtful." But this rule cannot be followed when we are bound to do one of two things, as to each of which we are equally in doubt. We are then entitled to choose that which we consider to be the less unjust; for always, where choice cannot be avoided, the lesser evil takes the character of the good. . . .

IV. (1) But to judge rightly, some skill and experience is necessary; and those who are without such ought to take the advice of wise men in order rightly to form their active judgment. . . .

VI. War is a matter of gravest importance, because so many calamities usually follow in its train, even upon the head of the innocent. So, where counsels conflict we ought to incline towards peace. . . . And there are three ways by which disputes can be settled without recourse to war.

VII. (1) The first is by a Conference. "There being two kinds of disputation," says Cicero, "the one by reasoning and the other by force, and the former being the peculiar method of mankind and the latter of brutes, the way of the brute is to be followed only when that of humanity is impossible." . . .

VIII. (1) The second is by Arbitration. "It is wicked," says Thucydides, "to fall upon him as an enemy who is willing to

refer his case to an arbitrator." . . . (3) But much more are
Christian kings and States obliged to adopt this method of
avoiding war. For if arbitrators were appointed both by Jews
and Christians in order to avoid litigation before pagan judges,
this practice, indeed, being expressly commanded by St. Paul,
how much more should this be done in order to avoid the much
greater inconvenience of war? . . . (4) And for this and other
reasons it would be convenient, and, indeed, it is almost necessary,
for congresses of Christian Powers to be held, where international
disputes could be settled by the disinterested Powers. Means
might be devised, indeed, to compel conflicting States to accept
a peace on reasonable terms. . . .

IX. The third is by lot. . . .

X. (1) Something like this is single combat. And it does not
seem that the practice of this ought to be repudiated altogether
if thereby two persons, whose quarrels would otherwise involve
two nations in the gravest misfortunes, are ready to come to a
mutual settlement by fighting one another. . . . For it seems that
such fighting, though not justifiable as between the parties themselves, may yet certainly be acquiesced in by the two nations
concerned as being the lesser evil. . . .

XI. But though in a doubtful case each party is bound to
endeavour to discover conditions by which war may be avoided,
yet he who makes a demand is more so bound than he who is
in actual possession. The maxim holds good in Natural Law,
as well as in the Civil Law, that " in all cases of equal claim he
who is in possession has presumably the better right." . . .

XII. Where, however, the right is doubtful, and neither is in
possession, or each is equally so, he shall be regarded as in the
wrong who refuses, when it is offered to him, a half of the matter
in question.

XIII. (1) From what we have said it is now possible to settle
that much controverted question whether a war, having regard
to the justification therefor of its principal authors, can be just
and lawful on both sides. . . . (2) In the particular acceptation
of justice, as relating to a particular act, a war can no more
have justice on both sides than can a matter in litigation, for
there cannot, by the nature of the act, be contradictory moral
claims in respect to it, as, for instance, that a certain act should

be done and also that it should not be done. Yet, nevertheless, it can clearly happen that neither belligerent act unjustly, for no one acts unjustly unless he knows that what he does is unjust; but many do not know that when it is so. Both parties to a dispute are able, accordingly, to litigate justly, that is to say, in good faith. For much, both of the law and of the facts determining the justice of a case, usually escapes the notice of the litigants. . . . (4) But as in war it rarely happens that there is not some rashness at the least or some lack of charity, the matter being so grave we should not be content with mere probabilities, but only with the most certain causes. (5) But if we understand the word " just " as involving certain juridical incidents, it is certain that in this sense a war may be just on both sides; as will appear from what we shall have to say about solemn public war. It is in this sense that an illegal sentence or wrongful possession has such incidents.

CHAPTER XXIV.—A WARNING NOT TO ENGAGE IN WARFARE RASHLY, EVEN FOR JUST CAUSE.

I. (1) Though it might appear to be foreign to our subject, which is the Rights or Justice of War, to explain what other virtues than justice direct or advise as to the making of war, yet, incidentally, we must note a certain common error, lest anyone should consider that, where valid cause clearly exists, a war ought to be undertaken either immediately or at any other time that is convenient. It happens, indeed, on the contrary, that more often than not there is a greater humanity and morality in giving up one's rights. . . . This generosity is especially incumbent upon Christians, who are called upon to imitate in this regard the most perfect example of Christ, Who laid down His life for us when we were godless and His enemies. Here is an example which should so increase our generous impulses as to make us hesitate to assert our proprietary and other rights at the fearful cost to others which war involves. . . .

II. (3) . . . If Christ desired that we should undervalue certain interests rather than go to law, then without doubt He would have us indifferent to those greater interests that may lead to war, which is so much more pernicious than mere litigation. (4) " For a good man to relax something of his rights," says St. Ambrose, " is not only an act of generosity, but is often even one of convenience." [And so Aristides and Xenophon.]

III. (1) And as for punishment, it is our first duty, if not as men, then most certainly as Christians, readily and freely to condone the wrongs we suffer, as God in Christ condones our offences. . . . [So Seneca, Aristotle, and Cicero.] . . .

IV. (1) Often also it is to the interest of ourselves and our people to decline a war. . . . In one of His parables Christ says that if a king is about to make war against another he first sits down (the custom of those in anxious deliberation) and considers whether he is able with ten thousand men to meet an enemy

having twenty thousand, and finding that he has insufficient
strength sends an ambassador to treat for peace before the enemy
enters his territory. . . . (3) And it is possible to temporise, as,
according to Strabo, in the case of Syrmus, King of the Triballi.
Alexander the Great wishing to enter the Isle of Peuce, Syrmus
forbad him, but at the same time sent gifts to him in order to
show that his prohibition was prompted by a just fear and not
by hatred and contempt.

V. (1) Those who deliberate in such cases consider partly the
ends—not the ultimate, but the subordinate ends—and partly the
means to those ends. And the end is always some good, or, at
least, the avoidance of some evil, which is much the same thing.
The means are not sought for themselves, but according as they
lead to an end. And so in our deliberations we must not only
compare the ends with one another but the means with their
effectiveness to accomplish the required ends. . . . Three rules
are to be observed in making these comparisons. (2) This is the
first rule. If the matter in question appears, morally speaking, to
be equally effective for good and for evil, it is to be undertaken
only if the good result has in it more of good than the evil result
has of evil. . . . (3) The second rule is, that if it appears that
good and evil may equally result from the matter in question,
it must be chosen only if its tendency is more to good than to
evil. And thirdly. If the good and evil appear to be unequal, the
effectiveness for either being no less unequal, we may still venture
upon the matter if its effectiveness for good as compared with
its effectiveness for evil is greater than the evil as compared
with the good, or if the good as compared with the evil is greater
than the effectiveness for evil compared with the effectiveness
for good. (4) All this, perhaps, is a little too subtle. But Cicero
expresses the same idea a little more plainly when he says that
" we are to avoid rushing into danger without cause, than which
there is nothing more foolish." . . .

VI. (2) But right reason suggests something quite different—
that life is of more value than liberty, for it is the foundation of
all temporal good and the occasion of all eternal happiness, and
this whether you consider it either in relation to an individual
or to a whole people. And so God Himself regards it as a
benefit that He does not destroy men, but delivers them into

slavery. . . . (3) The destruction of a people, in such circumstances, ought to be regarded as the greatest of evils. . . . (5) And what I have said of liberty I would have understood of other desirable things—they should be sacrificed if there otherwise would be a more, or even equally, justifiable fear of a greater mischief. For, as Aristides well says, to save a ship it is the custom to throw overboard the cargo, and not the passengers.

VII. It must also be especially observed that no war should be undertaken, with a view to inflicting punishment, against a nation of equal strength. For as a civil magistrate ought to be more powerful than the criminal, so ought he who seeks to punish misdeeds by war be more powerful than the one he attacks. Not only does prudence, or consideration for his own people, usually require that a Sovereign should refrain from hazardous warfare, but frequently even justice—that is to say, political justice— which, from the very nature of his sovereignty, demands no less of him a consideration for his subjects than of them their obedience to him. Wherefore it results, as theologians have rightly concluded, that a king who wages a war for slight cause, or to inflict needless punishment, thereby involving his subjects in a very hazardous adventure, is bound to recompense them for the injuries they suffer thereby. For though he has not injured his enemy yet he has done his subjects a grave wrong by plunging them in so much misfortune upon such an account. . . . As Ovid says, " Let the soldier bear only those arms with which he can put down arms."

VIII. Rare, then, is that cause of war which cannot, or ought not to be disregarded—that " cause which," as Florus says, " is more savage and unendurable than war itself." And Seneca says that " we may run into danger when we have as much," or more, " to fear if we sit still." . . .

IX. Another time for going to war is when, upon just estimation, we have right on our side, and also what is of greatest consequence—the power to maintain that right. . . .

X. (1) " War is a savage business," says Plutarch, " and brings in its train an infinity of injuries and violence." And St. Augustine very wisely says : ". . . To fight is the happiness of the wicked, but the necessity of the good. . . ." And Maximus Tyrius : " War is quite certainly not undertaken by

5*

the just unless it is necessary, though the unjust plunge into it
for mere choice." . . . (3) If, according to the Jewish law, he
who had slain a man, even though by accident, was forced to
fly; if God forbad David to build His temple, because he had
shed much blood, even though his wars are said to have been
just; if among the ancient Greeks they who had stained their
hands with human blood, though without fault, had need of
expiation—who, especially a Christian, can fail to see how unhappy
and very evil a thing is war, and how strenuously we ought to
avoid it, even though not unjust? And it is certain that among
the Greek Christians a canon was long observed, by which those
who had slain an enemy in any war whatever were for a time
excommunicated.

CHAPTER XXV.—OF THE CAUSES FOR WHICH WAR MAY BE UNDERTAKEN ON BEHALF OF OTHERS.

I. (1) Above, when we dealt with those who have the right to make war, we stated and proved that, by Natural Law, every man has authority not only to maintain his own rights but also those of others. And so, whatever causes justify a man making war on his own account, also justify him who fights in aid of another. (2) But our first and chief care should be those who are under our protection and power, whether in a family or State, for, as we showed, such are a part, as it were, of our political personality. So the Hebrews took up arms, under Joshua, on behalf of the Gibeonites, who had become their political dependents. . . .

II. Yet not always is the political superior bound to make war on behalf of his dependent, even though the cause be just. He is bound only if he can so act without inconvenience to all, or the greater part, of his subjects; for it is the business of a ruler to consider the interests of the whole of his people rather than those of a part. And the greater the part, the nearer it approaches the nature of the whole.

IV. Next to subjects, or, indeed, equally with them, we ought to defend our allies when there is an engagement for defence in the treaty of alliance; and this, whether they have placed themselves entirely under our protection or the treaty is one of mutual help. . . .

V. A third reason for war is the protection of our friends, that is to say, of those to whom, though no express promise of help has been given, assistance is due, as it were, because of friendship, if it can be given without too great effort and inconvenience. . . .

VI. The last and widest reason is the solidarity of mankind, and this alone is sufficient. "Men are born for mutual help," observes Seneca. . . . And, according to St. Ambrose, "that courage which defends the weak is the most perfect Justice."

VII. (1) Here the question arises whether a man or a nation is under obligation to defend from injury any other man or nation respectively. Plato even thinks that he should be punished who does not repel a violence offered to another; and such was the law of the Egyptians. But in the first place, where there is manifest danger there is no such obligation, for everyone is entitled to prefer his own life and property to those of others. . . . (2) And the opinion of Seneca should not be ignored: " I will help any man who is perishing, if I can do it without perishing myself; unless my ruin is to be the ransom of some great man or great cause." But even then he is not bound to help if the person threatened cannot be delivered without the death of the assailant. For if, as we have said, the victim may value the life of the assailant more than his own, the third party will not be to blame if he believes, or chooses to believe, that the person threatened prefers to perish, especially as the assailant runs a greater risk of irreparable and eternal damnation.

VIII. (1) There is also the question whether the delivery of a people from its ruler's oppression is a just cause for war. True it is that from the first institution of civil societies the rulers of each have claimed some special right over their own subjects. . . . (2) But the question is not very doubtful if oppression is manifest; for if a Busiris, a Phalaris, or a Diomede of Thrace should oppress his subjects to an extent that no just man could approve, there would still exist that primal right born of human solidarity. So Constantine took up arms against Maxentius and Licinius; and other Roman emperors took, or threatened to take, up arms against the Persians, unless they ceased to persecute the Christians on account of their religion alone. (3) Yes, though it be granted that subjects cannot lawfully take up arms against their rulers even in circumstances of extreme necessity (as to which, as we have seen, even those self-appointed champions of regal power are doubtful), yet it does not therefore follow that others cannot take up arms on their behalf. For whenever the obstacle to an action is in the actor, and not in the act itself, then what is not permitted to one may be lawful for another on his behalf, if only it is something in which one man may help another. So a guardian may litigate for a minor, who cannot himself do so; and for an absent party one may plead even without specific authority. But the prohibition against resistance by a subject does not arise because of the cause of his disaffection, which is the same in relation both to himself and a non-subject, but from his quality of subject, which does not pass to others.

IX. (3) War is not one of the social arts. Rather, it is something so horrible that only sheer necessity or perfect charity can make it lawful. . . .

CHAPTER XXVI.—OF THE JUST CAUSES FOR WHICH THOSE UNDER THE AUTHORITY OF ANOTHER MAY ENGAGE IN WAR.

I. So far we have dealt with those who are their own masters. But there are others who are in circumstances of obedience or subjection, such as sons of families, servants, subjects, and even individual citizens, as compared with the whole body of the State.

II. These, if they are consulted on the matter, or if they are given a free choice of war or peace, ought to follow the same rules as do those who, by their own authority, engage in war for themselves or others.

III. (1) But if they are commanded to fight, which is usually the case, they ought to abstain altogether if they are clear that the war is for an unjust cause. We are told, not only by the Apostles, but even by Socrates, that we should rather obey God than man. . . . (4) Josephus relates from Hecataeus that the Jews who bore arms under Alexander the Great could not be compelled, either by whips or by any degradations, to co-operate with the rest of his soldiers in banking up earth for the restoration of the Temple of Belus at Babylon. But we have an instance nearer to our argument in the Theban Legion, of which we have already spoken. . . . (5) The rule is the same if anyone is but merely persuaded that what he is ordered to do is unjust; for to him the thing is unlawful so long as he cannot get rid of that opinion, as appears from what has been said above.

IV. (1) But if the subject is doubtful whether or not the cause is lawful, must he remain quiet or fight? The general opinion is that he should fight. Nor should that celebrated maxim, " Act not at all in a doubtful case," prevent him, for he who hesitates in mere speculation may have no hesitation in practice. He may, indeed, believe that in doubtful matters he should obey his superiors. Nor can it be disputed that this distinction of the judgment into speculative and practical undoubtedly obtains in

many cases. The Civil Law, not only of Rome but of other
nations, not only concedes that he who is obedient in such circumstances is not to be punished but it even refuses a civil action
against him. According to that law, he commits the wrong who
orders it to be done; he is guilty of no fault who is bound to
obey; the necessity imposed by a superior excuses; and the like.
(2) . . . "A servant," says Seneca, "is not the critic, but the
minister, of his master's commands." (3) And St. Augustine,
in his opinion on this matter of military service, is very precise
in the same sense. . . . And hence it is the universal opinion
that, as regards subjects, a war may be just on both sides, that
is to say, free from injustice. . . . (4) Yet this matter is not
without its own difficulty. Adrian, the last Cisalpine Pope,
maintained the contrary, which, though it cannot be precisely
supported on his reasoning, may be more convincingly put on this
—that he who doubts in speculation ought, in practice, to choose
the safer side. And the safer side is to abstain from war. . . .
(7) As a fact, as we shall presently show, declarations of war are
usually made publicly, stating the cause of the war, so that all
mankind, as it were, may be able to judge as to its justice.
Prudence, according to Aristotle, is a virtue peculiar to a prince,
but justice belongs to every man as such. But it would seem
that the above opinion of Adrian ought to be absolutely relied
on only if the subject not merely doubts as to the justice of the
cause, but, induced by more probable arguments, is more inclined
to believe that the war is unjust, especially if it is a question
of an offensive war as distinguished from a war of defence.

V. (1) If, however, it is impossible, by exposition of the cause
of a war, to satisfy the consciences of all his subjects, it is the
clear duty of a good prince rather to subject them to special
taxation than to military service—especially when there are others
ready to serve. And these latter may be made use of by a just
prince, whether their intentions are good or evil—as even God
sometimes makes use of the acts of the Devil and of the wicked—
on the same principle that absolves from fault the poverty-driven
wretch who takes the money of a voracious usurer. (2) Yes,
though the justice of the war cannot be in doubt, yet, nevertheless, it does not seem at all right that Christians should be forced,
against their will, into military service. And this is so because

abstention from military service, even when such service is permissible, is conduct of that greater holiness which for a long time has been required of the clergy and penitents and is strongly approved in many ways, for other Christians. . . .

VI. (1) Still, I am of opinion that it may happen that in a war not only doubtful, but even manifestly unjust, subjects may lawfully take up arms in their own defence.   For since the enemy, though carrying on a war which is just on his side, has not an absolute and inherent right to slay innocent subjects who have no concern with the cause of war on their side, unless it be either necessary for his defence or incidentally to the attainment of his end (for these subjects are not liable to punishment), it follows that, if it is certain that the enemy is falling upon them with intent not to give quarter, such subjects are allowed by Natural Law to defend themselves, and of this right they are not deprived by the Law of Nations.

BOOK III.

CHAPTER I.—GENERAL RULES FROM NATURAL LAW AS TO WHAT IS LAWFUL IN WAR; AND HEREIN OF DECEIT AND FALSEHOOD.

I. We have seen who may wage war and what causes justify war. We must now enquire into what is lawful in war, and to what extent and in what circumstances it is so; either simply itself or in relation to some antecedent · promise; and· simply, first from Natural Law, and then from the Law of Nations. Let us now see what Natural Law permits.

II. (1) First, as we have repeatedly said, all means to an end of a moral nature derive from that end itself an intrinsic worth; and so we may conclude that we have a right to use such means as are necessary, morally as distinguished from physically, for the assertion of our rights. And by " rights " I here mean what are strictly so called—the power of acting conformably to social interest alone. Wherefore, as we have elsewhere noted, if I am unable otherwise to preserve my life, I may, by any force whatever, repel him who threatens it; because this right does not properly arise from the wrongdoing of my assailant, but from Nature herself, who has invested me with the right to preserve myself. (2) And this same right also allows me to seize the property of another, if it threatens me with imminent danger, without considering whether its owner is in fault or not. Yet I do not thereby acquire ownership, for such is not a means necessary for the end in view, but only, as we have explained elsewhere, a right to hold it until my security is sufficiently provided for. So I have a natural right to retake possession of any property of mine that another wrongfully detains, or, if that is not easily done, to take something else of equal value; and I may do the like for the recovery of a debt; in which cases ownership itself follows, because by no other means could equality be restored. (3) So, when punishment is just, all force is just that is necessary to inflict the punishment, including everything that is part of the punishment, such as the destruction of property by fire or otherwise, provided it be within just limits and proportionate to the offence committed.

III. Secondly, it must be understood that our rights are not to be estimated by reference only to the first causes of the war, but also to new causes which come into existence during the course of the war; just as in litigation it often happens that a party acquires new rights after process has issued. Thus, those who join forces with the enemy, whether allies or subjects, give me the right of defending myself against them also. So those who take part in an unjust war, especially if they might or ought to know that it is unjust, become bound thereby to make good the expense and damage of it, because such are the consequences of their own wrongdoing. So, too, those who come into a war begun without a good reason thereby render themselves liable to a punishment proportionate to the injustice involved in their action. . . .

IV. (1) It should be observed, thirdly, that the right to do a thing imports a permission consequentially to do many things indirectly and without deliberate intent, even to do things which *per se* could not be lawfully done. How this holds good in the case of self-defence we have elsewhere shown. So, in order to recover our own, if we cannot take precisely our due we have a right to take more, subject, however, to an obligation to restore the value of the excess. And thus you may bombard a ship filled with pirates or a house full of thieves, although there may be in the ship or house a few infants or women or other innocent persons who may thus be exposed to danger. . . . (2) But, as we have frequently pointed out before, that which is conformable to strict right is not always absolutely lawful, for sometimes charity to our neighbour does not permit us to enforce that right. Therefore any acts incidental to those we have planned, and which can be foreseen, ought to be avoided, unless—according as only prudence can determine—the good which may result therefrom be far greater than the evil to be feared, or unless, the good and evil being equal, there is far greater expectation of good than fear of evil. Moreover, in a doubtful case, we must always, for safety's sake, regard the interests of others rather than our own.

V. (1) Here another question usually arises : What may we lawfully do against those who, not being our enemies, or not wishing to be regarded as such, yet provide our enemies with various supplies? And this question has been quite bitterly debated, not only in the past, but quite recently, some contending for the rigour of war and others for the freedom of commerce. (2) But first we must distinguish between the things themselves. There are some things which are useful only in war, such as arms; some which are of no use at all in war, such as those which serve only for pleasure; and some which are of use both for war and in peace, such as money, provisions, and ships and marine stores. Concerning the first kind, that is true which Amalasuintha said to Justinian—that they who supply the enemy with necessaries of war are part of his side. As to the second kind, no question can arise. . . . (3) As to the third class, being articles of doubtful use, the actual state of the war must be considered. For if I am unable to defend myself unless I intercept those things when in transit, necessity, as we have elsewhere explained, will justify their seizure, subject, of course, to an obligation to restore them if there is no cause to the contrary. Because if their delivery to the enemy will hinder the enforcement of my rights, and the sender can know that—as if I were besieging a town or blockading a port, and surrender or peace was expected—he is liable to me for damages, just as anyone would be who should release my debtor from prison or help him to escape in order to cheat me. And I may seize his goods proportionately to the damage I have suffered, and assume their ownership in order to satisfy my claim. If, however, he has not yet done the damage, but is only about to do it, I have the right to hold the goods in order to compel him to give security for the future—by hostages, by pledge, or in other ways. If, moreover, the injustice of my enemy's cause is obvious and clear, and the sender thus encourages him in a most unjust war, he is then liable, not only civilly but even criminally, for the damage he does me, as one who rescues a notorious offender from the hands of justice ; and on that ground measures appropriate to his offence may be taken against him, in accordance with the rules we have already set down for punishments, and so, subject to those principles, we may even pillage him. (4) **And** on this account it is usual directly a war is commenced for the belligerents to publish, for the information of other nations, a statement both disclosing the justice of their cause and also what probable hope they have of enforcing their rights. . . .

VI. (1) As to the mode of waging war, force and terror are the most appropriate means. But may stratagem also be employed? This is a quite common question. Homer answers in the affirmative: " The enemy is to be injured, no matter whether by fraud or force, openly or concealed." . . . And so [others and] (2) Ammianus: " Without any distinction between courage and craft, all successful efforts in war ought to be glorified." (3) The Roman jurists called a fraud " good " if used against an enemy, and also said that it mattered not if a man baffled his enemy by force or by fraud. So Eustathius: " Deceit is not to be blamed, as belonging to a soldier." And among the theologians there is St. Augustine, who says that " if the war be just it concerns not justice whether one fights openly or by stratagem," and St. Chrysostom remarks that emperors who secure victory by fraud are most to be commended. (4) Yet we are not without opinions which seem to maintain the contrary, of which I shall mention some presently. The real point, however, is this: Is fraud, merely as such, always an evil? If so, then we must not do evil in order that good may come. If not so, then the question is whether the act in contemplation, not being inherently and universally evil, may not, as it may sometimes happen, be good in the particular circumstances.

CHAPTER XV.—MODERATION IN CONQUEST.

I. What equity requires, or humanity commends, to be shown towards individuals, is so much the more to be shown towards nations or parts of nations, inasmuch as wrongs or kindness done to many is the more remarkable. As other things may be acquired in a just war, so may sovereignty over a nation and even the very sovereignty enjoyed by a nation itself, though only so far as can be justified as a punishment for wrongdoing or a satisfaction of some obligation. To which may be added—or in order to avoid some grave public danger. But though this justification is generally involved with others, yet it should be chiefly considered for its own sake both in concluding peace and in pressing a victory. For while other things may be remitted out of pity, in a grave public danger any pity which disregards the demands of safety is nothing else than cruelty. Isocrates tells Philip that "the barbarians should be subdued so far as to place his own country in safety."

II. (1) And Sallust said of the ancient Romans: "Our ancestors, most religious of men, took nothing from the vanquished except liberty to do wrong"—words worthy of a Christian, and which agree with another of his sayings—that "wise men make war for the sake of peace, and labour in the hope of rest." . . . (2) And none of this is inconsistent with the teaching of Christian theologians, that the object of war is to remove obstacles to peace. And before the time of Ninus, as we have already quoted from Trogus, it was the custom to maintain the boundaries of empire rather than to extend them: everyone's rule ended with his own country; and kings did not seek power for themselves, but glory for their peoples, and, satisfied with victory, abstained from empire. To this state St. Augustine brings us back, as much as he can, when he says: "Let them consider that it is not for good men to rejoice in the extent of their dominion," and adds: "It is a greater happiness to have a good neighbour at peace than to subdue a bad one by war." And the prophet

Amos severely rebukes the Ammonites for their anxiety to extend
their territories by force of arms.

III. The prudent moderation of the old Romans comes very
near to this example of primitive innocence. "What to-day would
our empire have been," asks Seneca, "if a wholesome prudence
had not mingled the conquerors with the conquered?" "And,"
says Claudius in Tacitus, "our founder Romulus was so wise
that most of his enemies became citizens within a day." . . .
Lastly, what is very wonderful, all people under the sway of
Rome were made citizens of Rome by a decree of the Emperor
Antonine. For this we have the authority of Ulpian. So, as
Modestinus observes, Rome was called *Communis Patria*—the
common country. And, to quote Claudian, "We owe this happy
union of so many diverse peoples to Rome's persistent policy
of peace."

IV. (1) Another kind of moderation in victory is to leave their
own government to the conquered, whether sovereigns or peoples.
. . . (2) So the Romans permitted the Cappadocians to have
what form of government they would. And many nations were
left free after war . . . [it being] the custom of Rome to spare
the vanquished, for "the greatest souls are the most generous
in victory." In Tacitus we read that "nothing was taken from
Zorsines when he was conquered." . . .

V. Still, regard must be had for the security of the conqueror
when power is being conceded to the conquered. . . .

VI. So it may often happen that tribute is imposed in order
to provide not so much for reparation as for the future security of
both conqueror and conquered. . . .

VII. (1) But that their own government should be left to the
conquered is not only a measure of humanity but often also one
of policy. . . .

IX. If, however, it be not safe to leave the conquered their
liberty, yet some moderation may be possible, as, for instance,
their kings or a part of their own government may be left to
them. . . .

X. And even when they are entirely deprived of their own
government they may be allowed to retain their ordinary laws,
with regard to public and private matters, and also their own
customs and magistrates. . . .

XI. (1) Another privilege which may be granted to the conquered is the enjoyment of their national religion, unless they
can be persuaded to change it. . . . (2) But if their religion is
a false one, then the conqueror will take care that the true religion
shall not be oppressed. . . .

XII. (1) My last advice is this—that however complete and
absolute be the power which the conquerors have obtained, the
conquered should be treated with clemency, in order that the
interests of each may become the interest of both. . . . (2) The
Privernian ambassador, being asked in the Roman Senate what
peace the Romans might expect from his people, replied: " If
you grant us a good peace, it will be sure and permanent; if
bad, it will not last long." And he gives the reason: " You
cannot believe that any nation, or even any individual, can remain
any longer than is necessary in a condition that does not satisfy
him." So, according to Camillus, that government is most secure
where the subjects are glad to obey. And the Scythians told
Alexander: " There is no friendship between lord and slave, for
though they live in peace the laws of war remain." And
Hermocratus, in Diodorus, declares that it is not so glorious a
thing to conquer as to use victory with clemency. The saying
of Tacitus is very applicable in regard to the use of victory:
" Excellent are the conclusions of those wars where pardons are
the characteristic of the final terms." And, lastly, there is the
letter of the dictator Cæsar: " Let this be a new way of
conquering: to protect ourselves by mercy and generosity."

CHAPTER XXV.—THE CONCLUSION, WITH ADMONI-
TIONS TO GOOD FAITH AND PEACE.

I. (1) And here, I think, I may make an end. Not that I
have said all that might have been said, but that what has been
said may be enough to lay the foundations; so that if anyone
will build thereon a fairer fabric, far from envying, I shall be
heartily grateful to him. Yet before I dismiss the reader I will
add a few admonitions which may tend, both during and after
war, to the preservation of good faith and peace, as, when I
was speaking of the launching of war, I added some arguments
with a view to any possible prevention of war. And I am anxious
for good faith especially, lest all hope of peace be taken away,
as well as for other reasons. For, according to Cicero, not only
is each State held together by good faith, but even that greater
society of nations. And Aristotle truly says that if this be taken
away all human intercourse ceases. (2) . . . And this should
be the more carefully kept by Sovereigns, as they enjoy greater
impunity than others in its violation. For once good faith disappears they will become like wild beasts, whose violence all men
dread. Then, too, while the other attributes of justice are somewhat obscure, that of good faith is so obvious as even to be used
in all the dealings of men in order to remove obscurity. (3) How
much more ought Sovereigns to observe good faith—first, for
the sake of their conscience; and secondly, for the sake of their
reputation, upon which stands the authority of kingdoms. Let
them not doubt, then, that politicians who instil into them the
principles of deceit do themselves practise what they teach. And
principles cannot prosper long which render men not only unfit
for human association, but even hateful to God.

II. Further, no mind can remain serene and faithful to God
throughout the whole conduct of a war unless it ever looks
forward to peace. For it has been very truly said by Sallust

that "wise men wage war for the sake of peace," an opinion in harmony with that of St. Augustine: "We do not seek peace in order to wage war, but we wage war in order to secure peace"; and Aristotle often condemns those nations that make war their main and ultimate object as it were. There is a certain brutal violence which is most prominent in war; and therefore it ought to be most carefully contrived that war is tempered by humanity, lest we forget our manhood in an overmuch imitation of beasts.

III. If, then, a sufficiently safe peace can be secured by the condonation of evildoers, damages, and expenses, it is not a bad settlement, especially between Christians, to whom our Lord gave His peace as a last legacy. So St. Paul, best of His expositors, would have us live peaceably with all men, so far as in us lies. And, as we read in Sallust, " a good man enters into a war with regret, and does not willingly prosecute it to extremes."

IV. All this ought to be enough. But even human interests often draw men in the same direction—first, those who are the weakest. For a long struggle with a more powerful opponent is full of danger; and anger and hope (deceitful advisers!) should be disregarded, just as, at sea, a greater misfortune is averted by throwing something overboard. . . .

V. And then there are those who are the more powerful. As Livy most truly says, peace is glorious and beneficial when granted by those whose circumstances are prosperous, and is more advantageous and more permanent than a merely anticipatory victory. . . . And the courage of despair, like the sharp teeth of dying beasts, is especially to be feared.

VI. But what if both parties seem to be of equal strength? Then, according to Cæsar, the best time to conclude peace is whilst each party trusts in his own strength.

VII. But peace having once been made, no matter upon what conditions, ought to be most strictly kept, because of the sanctity of that which we have called good faith; and not only should perfidy be most carefully avoided, but anything which may exasperate our opponent's mind. For what Cicero has said about private friendships is no less fitly applicable to public—that as all friendships are to be preserved most religiously and faithfully, so especially should those which have resolved a state of war into a happy peace.

VIII. May, then, the Almighty, Who alone can do it, inscribe these lessons in the hearts of those who control the affairs of Christendom; and may He enlighten their minds with a sense of justice, both human and divine; and may He lead them ever to feel that they are His chosen ministers for the government of Man—the dearest of His creatures.

Printed at Reading, England, by the Eastern Press, Ltd.

AN ESSAY

TOWARDS THE PRESENT AND FUTURE

PEACE OF EUROPE

BY WILLIAM PENN.

FIRST PUBLISHED IN 1693-94.

WASHINGTON, D. C.
THE AMERICAN PEACE SOCIETY.
1912.

Beati Pacifici.

An Essay towards the Present and Future Peace of Europe, by the Establishment of an European Dyet, Parliament, or Estates.

Beati Pacifici.   Cedant arma togae.

To the Reader:

I have undertaken a Subject that I am very sensible re-quires one of more sufficiency than I am Master of to treat it, as, in Truth, it deserves, and the groaning State of Eu-rope calls for; but since Bunglers may Stumble upon the Game, as well as Masters, though it belongs to the Skilful to hunt and catch it. I hope this Essay will not be charged upon me for a Fault, if it appear to be neither Chimerical nor Injurious, and may provoke abler Pens to improve and perform the Design with better Judgment and Success. I will say no more in Excuse of myself, for this Undertak-ing, but that it is the Fruit of my solicitous Thoughts, for the Peace of Europe, and they must want Charity as much as the world needs Quiet, to be offended with me for so Pa-cifick a Proposal. Let them censure my Management, so they prosecute the Advantage of the Design; for 'till the Millenary Doctrine be accomplished, there is nothing appears to me so beneficial an Expedient to the Peace and Happiness of this Quarter of the World.

AN ESSAY TOWARDS THE PRESENT AND FUTURE PEACE OF
EUROPE, &c.

Sect. I.   *Of Peace, and its Advantages.*

He must not be a Man but a Statue of Brass or Stone, whose Bowels do not melt when he beholds the bloody *Tragedies* of this War, in *Hungary, Germany, Flanders, Ireland*, and at Sea: The Mortality of sickly and lan-guishing Camps and Navies, and the mighty prey the De-vouring Winds and Waves have made upon Ships and

Men since 88. And as this with Reason ought to affect
human Nature, and deeply Kindred, so there is something
very moving that becomes prudent Men to consider, and
that is the vast Charge that has accompanied that Blood,
and which makes no mean Part of these *Tragedies;* Especially if they deliberate upon the uncertainty of the
War, that they know not how or when it will end, and
that the Expense cannot be less, and the Hazard is as
great as before. So that in the Contraries of Peace we
see the Beauties and Benefits of it; which under it, such
is the Unhappiness of Mankind, we are too apt to nau-
seate, as the full Stomach loaths the Honey-Comb; and
like that unfortunate Gentleman, that having a fine and
a good Woman to his Wife, and searching his Pleasure
in forbidden and less agreeable Company, said, when reproach'd with his Neglect of better Enjoyments, *That he
could love his Wife of all Women, if she were not his Wife,*
tho' that increased his Obligation to prefer her. It is a
great Mark of the Corruption of our Natures, and what
ought to humble us extremely, and excite the Exercise of
our Reason to a nobler and juster Sense, that we cannot
see the Use and Pleasure of our Comforts but by the
Want of them. As if we could not taste the Benefit of
Health, but by the Help of Sickness; nor understand the
Satisfaction of Fulness without the Instruction of Want;
nor, finally, know the Comfort of Peace, but by the
Smart and Penance of the Vices of War: And without
Dispute that is not the least Reason that God is pleased
to Chastise us so frequently with it. What can we desire
better than *Peace*, but the *Grace* to use it? *Peace* pre-
serves our Possessions; We are in no Danger of In-
vasions: Our Trade is free and Safe, and we rise and
lye down without Anxiety. The Rich bring out their
Hoards, and employ the poor Manufacturers; Buildings
and divers Projections, for Profit and Pleasure, go on:
It excites Industry, which brings Wealth, as that gives
the Means of Charity and Hospitality, not the lowest
ornaments of a Kingdom or Commonwealth. But War,
like the Frost of 83, seizes all these Comforts at once,
and stops the civil Channel of Society. The Rich draw
in their Stock, the Poor turn Soldiers, or Thieves, or

starve : No Industry, no Building, no Manufactory, little Hospitality or Charity ; but what the Peace gave, the
War devours. I need say no more upon this Head, when
the Advantages of Peace, and Mischiefs of War, are so
many and sensible to every Capacity under all Governments, as either of them prevails. I shall proceed to
the next Point. *What is the best Means of Peace;* which
will conduce much to open my Way to what I have to
propose.

SECT. II. *Of the Means of Peace, which is Justice
rather than War.*

As *Justice* is a Preserver, so it is a better Procurer of
Peace than War. Tho' *Pax quaeritur bello* be an usual
Saying, *Peace is the end of War,* and as such it was taken
up by O. C. for his Motto ; Yet the Use generally made
of that expression shews us, that properly and truly
speaking, Men seek their Wills by *War* rather than
Peace, and that as they will violate it to obtain them, so
they will hardly be brought to think of Peace, unless their
Appetites be some Way gratified. If we look over the
Stories of all Times, we shall find the Aggressors generally moved by Ambition ; the Pride of Conquest and
Greatness of Dominion more than Right. But as those
Leviathans appear rarely in the World, so I shall anon
endeavor to make it evident they had never been able to
devour the Peace of the World, and ingross whole Countries as they have done, if the *Proposal* I have to make
for the Benefit of our present Age had been then in
Practice. The Advantage that Justice has upon War is
seen by the Success of *Embassies,* that so often prevent
War by hearing the *Pleas* and *Memorials* of *Justice* in
the Hands and Mouths of the *Wronged Party.* Perhaps it
may be in a good Degree owing to *Reputation* or *Poverty,*
or some Particular *Interest* or *Conveniency* of *Princes* and
States, as much as *Justice;* but it is certain, that as War
cannot in any Sense be justified, but upon Wrongs received, and Right, upon Complaint, refused ; So the Generality of Wars have their Rise from some such Pretension
This is better seen and understood at Home ; for that
which prevents a Civil War in a Nation, is that which

4

may prevent it Abroad, viz: *Justice;* and we seé where
that is notably obstructed, War is kindled between the
Magistrates and *People* in particular Kingdoms and
States; which, however it may be unlawful on the side
of the *People*, we see never fails to follow, and ought to
give the same Caution to Princes, as if it were the Right
of the People to do it: Tho' I must needs say, *the
Remedy is almost ever worse than the Disease:* The Aggressors seldom getting what they seek, or performing,
if they prevail, what they promised: And the *Blood and
Poverty* that usually attend the Enterprise, weigh more
on Earth, as well as in Heaven, than what they lost or
suffered, or what they get by endeavoring to mend their
Condition, comes to: Which *Disappointment* seems to
be the Voice of Heaven, and Judgment of God against
those violent Attempts. But to return, I say, *Justice is
the Means of Peace,* betwixt the *Government* and the
People, and one *Man* and *Company* and another. It
prevents *Strife,* and at last ends it: For besides *Shame*
or *Fear,* to contend longer, he or they being under *Government,* are constrained to bound their *Desires* and *Re-
sentment* with the *Satisfaction* the Law gives. Thus
Peace is maintained by *Justice,* which is a Fruit of *Government,* as *Government* is from *Society,* and *Society* from
Consent.

SECT. III.   *Government, its Rise and End under all
Models.*

Government is an Expedient against *Confusion;* a Restraint upon all *Disorder;* Just Weights and an even Bal-
ance: That one may not injure another, nor himself, by
Intemperance.

This was at first without *Controversie, Patrimonial,* and
upon the Death of the Father or Head of the Family, the
eldest Son or Male of Kin succeeded. But Time break-
ing in upon this Way of Governing, as the World multi-
ply'd, it fell under other *Claims* and *Forms;* and is as
hard to trace to its Original, as are the Copies we have of
the first Writings of *Sacred* or *Civil* Matters. It is certain the most Natural and Human is that of *Consent,* for
that binds freely, (as I may say) when Men hold their

Liberty by true *Obedience* to Rules of their own making. No Man is Judge in his own Cause, which ends the *Confusion* and *Blood* of so many *Judges* and *Executioners*. For out of *Society* every Man is his own *King*, does what he lists at his own Peril : But when he comes to incorporate himself, he submits that *Royalty* to the *Conveniency* of the *Whole*, from whom he receives the Returns of *Protection*. So that he is not now his own Judge nor Avenger, neither is his *Antagonist*, but the *Law*, in indifferent Hands between both. And if he be Servant to others that before was free, he is also served of others that formerly owed him no *Obligation*. Thus while we are not our own, every Body is ours, and we get more than we lose, the Safety of the *Society* being the Safety of the *Particulars* that constitute it. So that while we seem to submit to, and hold all we have from *Society*, it is by *Society* that we keep what we have.

Government then is the *Prevention* or *Cure* of *Disorder*, and the Means of *Justice*, as that is of *Peace:* For this Cause they have *Sessions, Terms, Assizes,* and *Parliaments*, to overrule Men's *Passions* and *Resentments*, that they may not be *Judges* in their own *Cause*, nor *Punishers of* their own *Wrongs,* which, as it is very incident to *Men* in their *Corrupt State,* so, for that Reason, they would observe no Measure ; nor on the other Hand would any be easily reduced to their Duty. Not that Men know not what is right, their Excesses, and wherein they are to blame, by no Means ; nothing is plainer to them : But so depraved is Human Nature, that without Compulsion some Way or other, too many would not readily be brought to do what they know is right and fit, or avoid what they are satisfy'd they should not do : Which brings me near to the Point I have undertaken ; and for the better Understanding of which, I have thus briefly treated of *Peace, Justice,* and *Government.* as a necessary *Introduction,* because the Ways and Methods by which *Peace* is preserved in particular *Governments*, will help those *Readers* most concerned in my *Proposal* to conceive with what Ease as well as advantage the Peace of *Europe* might be procured and Kept; which is the End designed by me, with all Submission to those Interested in this little *Treatise.*

SECT. IV. *Of a General Peace, or the Peace of Europe, and the Means of it.*

In my first Section, I showed the *Desirableness of Peace;* in my next, the Truest Means of it; to wit, *Justice not War.* And in my last, that this Justice was the Fruit of *Government,* as Government itself was the Result of *Society* which first came from a Reasonable Design in Men of Peace. Now if the *Soveraign Princes of Europe,* who represent that Society, or Independent State of Men that was previous to the Obligations of Society, would, for the same Reason that engaged Men first into Society, *viz: Love of Peace and Order,* agree to meet by their Stated Deputies in a *General Dyet, Estates,* or *Parliament,* and there Establish Rules of Justice for Soveraign Princes to observe one to another; and thus to meet Yearly, or once in Two or Three Years at farthest, or as they shall see Cause. and to be stiled, *The Soveraign or Imperial Dyet, Parliament, or State of Europe;* before which Soveraign Assembly, should be brought all Differences depending between one Soveraign and another, that can not be made up by private Embassies, before the Sessions begin; and that if any of the Soveraignties that Constitute these Imperial States, shall refuse to submit their Claim or Pretensions to them, or to abide and perform the Judgment thereof, and seek their Remedy by Arms, or delay their Compliance beyond the Time prefixt in their Resolutions, all the other Soveraignties, United as One Strength, shall compel the Submission and Performance of the Sentence, with Damages to the Suffering Party, and Charges to the Soveraignties that obliged their Submission. To be sure, *Europe* would quietly obtain the so much desired and needed Peace, to *Her harassed Inhabitants;* no Soveraignty in *Europe* having the Power and therefore can not show the Will to dispute the Conclusion; and, consequently, *Peace* would be procured, and continued in *Europe.*

SECT. V. *Of the Causes of Difference, and Motives to Violate Peace.*

There appears to me but Three Things upon which Peace is broken, Viz: To *Keep,* to *Recover,* or to *Add.*

First, to Keep what is Ones Right, from the Invasion of an Enemy ; in which I am purely *Defensive*. *Secondly*. To Recover, when I think myself Strong enough, that which by Violence, I, or my Ancestors have lost by the Arms of a Stronger Power ; in which I am Offensive ; Or, *Lastly*, To increase my Dominion by the Acquisition of my Neighbour's Countries, as I find them Weak, and myself Strong. To gratify which Passion, there will never want some Accident or other for a Pretense : And Knowing my own Strength, I will be my own *Judge and Carver*. This *Last* will find no Room in the *Imperial States* : They are an unpassable Limit to that Ambition. But the other *Two* may come as soon as they please, and find the Justice of the Soveraign Court. And considering how few there are of those *Sons of Prey*. and how early they show themselves, it may be not once in an Age or Two, this Expedition being established, the Ballance can not well be broken.

SECT. VI. *Of Titles, upon which those Differences may arise.*

But I easily forsee a Question that may be answered in our Way, and that is this ; *What is Right ? Or else we can never know what is Wrong: It is very fit that this should be Established.* But that is fitter for the Soveraign States to resolve than me. And yet that I may lead a Way to the Matter, I say that Title is either by a long and *undoubted Succession*, as the Crowns of *Spain, France*, and *England;* or by *Election*, as the Crown of *Poland*, and the *Empire;* or by *Marriage*, as the Family of the *Stewarts* came by *England;* the *Electer of Brandenburg*, to the Dutchy of *Cleve:* and we, in Ancient Time, to divers Places abroad; or by Purchase, as hath been frequently done in *Italy* and *Germany;* or by Conquest, as the *Turk* in *Christendom*, the *Spaniards* in *Flanders*, formerly mostly in the *French* Hands and the *French* in *Burgundy, Normandy, Lorrain, French-County*, &c. This last Title is, Morally Speaking, only Questionable. It has indeed obtained a Place among the Rolls of Titles, but it was engross'd and recorded by the Point of the sword, and in Bloody Characters. What can not be con-

troubled or resisted, must be submitted to; but all the
World knows the Date of the length of such Empires,
and that they expire with the Power of the Possessor to
defend them. And yet there is a little allowed to Conquest too, when it has the Sanction of Articles of Peace
to confirm it : Tho' that hath not always extinguished the
Fire, but it lies, like Embers and Ashes, ready to Kindle
so soon as there is fit Matter prepared for it. Nevertheless, when Conquest has been confirmed by a Treaty, and
Conclusion of Peace, I must confess it is an Adopted
Title ; and if not so Genuine and Natural, yet being en-
grafted, it is fed by that which is the Security of *Better
Titles*, *Consent*. There is but one Thing more to be
mentioned in this Section, and that is from what Time
Titles shall take their Beginning, or how far back we
may look to confirm or dispute them. It would be very
bold and inexcusable in me, to determine so tender a
Point, but be it more or less Time, as to the last General
Peace at *Nimeguen*, or to the commencing of this War,
or to the Time of the Beginning of the Treaty of Peace, I
must submit it to the Great Pretenders and Masters in that
Affair. But something every Body must be willing to give
or quit, that he may keep the rest, and by this Establishment be forever freed of the Necessity of losing more.

SECT. VII. *Of the Composition of these Imperial States.*

The Composition and Proportion of this *Soveraign
Part*, or *Imperial State*, does, at the first Look, seem to
carry with it no small Difficulty what votes to allow for
the Inequality of the Princes and States. But with Submission to better Judgments, I can not think it invincible ;
For if it be possible to have an Estimate of the Yearly
Value of the several Soveraign Countries, whose Delegates are to make up this August Assembly, The Determination of the Number of Persons or Votes in the States
for every Soveraignty will not be impracticable. Now that
England, *France*, *Spain*, the *Empire*, &c., may be pretty
exactly estimated, is so plain a Case, by considering the
Revenue of Lands, the Exports and Entries at the Custom Houses, the Books of Rates, and Surveys that are in
all Governments, to proportion Taxes for the Support of

them, that the least Inclination to the *Peace of Europe*
will not stand or halt at this Objection. I will, with Par-
don on all Sides give an Instance far from Exact ; nor do
I pretend to it, or offer it for an Estimate ; for I do it at
Random : Only this, as wide as it is from the Just Proportion, will give some Aim to my *Judicious Reader*, what
I would be at : Remembering, I design not by any Computation, an Estimate from the Revenue of the Prince,
but the Value of the Territory, the Whole being concerned as well as the Prince. And a Juster Measure it
is to go by, since one Prince may have more Revenue
than another, who has much a Richer Country : Tho' in
the Instance I am now about to make, the Caution is not
so necessary, because, as I said before, I pretend to no
Manner of Exactness, but go wholly by Guess, being but
for Example's Sake. I suppose the *Empire of Germany*
to send Twelve ; *France*, Ten ; *Spain*, Ten ; *Italy*, which
comes to *France*, Eight ; *England*, Six ; *Portugal*, Three ;
Sweedland, Four ; *Denmark*, Three ; *Poland*, Four ; *Ven-
ice*, Three ; the *Seven Provinces*, Four ; *The Thirteen
Cantons*, and little *Neighbouring Soveraignties*, Two ;
Dukedoms of *Holstein* and *Courland*, One : And if the
Turks and *Muscovites* are taken in, as seems but fit and
just, they will make *Ten apiece more*. The *Whole* makes
Ninety. A great Presence when they represent the
*Fourth, and now The Best and Wealthiest Part of the
Known World ; where Religion and Learning, Civility and
Arts have their Seat and Empire*. But it is not absolutely necessary there should be always so many Persons,
to represent the larger Soveraignties ; for the Votes may
be given by one Man of any Soveraignty, as well as by
Ten or Twelve : Tho' the fuller the Assembly of States
is, the more Solemn, Effectual, and Free the Debates
will be, and the Resolutions must needs come with
greater Authority. The Place of their First Session
should be Central, as much as is possible, afterwards as
they agree.

SECT. VIII. *Of the Regulations of the Imperial States in
Session.*

To avoid Quarrel for Precedency, the Room may be

Round, and have divers Doors to come in and go out at, to prevent Exceptions. If the whole Number be cast in Tens, each chusing One, they may preside by Turns, to whom all Speeches should be addressed, and who chould collect the Sense of the Debates, and state the Question for a Vote, which, in my Opinion, should be by the *Ballot* after the Prudent and Commendable Method of the *Venetians:* Which, in a great Degree, prevents the ill Effects of Corruption; because if any of the Delegates of that High and Mighty Estates could be so Vile. False, and Dishonorable, as to be influenced by Money, they have the Advantage of taking their Money that will give it them and of Voting undiscovered to the Interest of their Principles, and their own Inclinations; as they that do understand the *Balloting Box* do very well know. A Shrewd Stratagem and an Experimental Remedy against *Corruption*, at least Corrupting: For who will give their Money where they may so easily be Cozened, and where it is Two to One they will be so; for they that will take Money in such Cases, will not stick to Lye heartly to them that give it, rather than wrong their Country, when they know their Lye can not be detected.

It seems to me, that nothing in this *Imperial Parliament* should pass, but by Three Quarters of the Whole, at least Seven above the Ballance. I am sure it helps to prevent Treachery, because if Money could ever be a Temptation in such a Court, it would cost a great Deal of Money to weigh down the wrong Scale. All Complaints should be delivered in Writing in the Nature of *Memorials* and *Journals* kept by a proper Person, in a *Trunk or Chest*, which should have as many differing Locks, *as there are Tens in the States*. And if there were a *Clerk for each Ten*, and a *Pew or Table for those Clerks in the Assembly;* and at the End of Every Session *One out of each Ten* were appointed to Examine and Compare the *Journal of those Clerks*, and then lock them up as I have before expressed. it would be clear and Satisfactory. And each Soveraignty if they please. as is but very fit, may have an *Exemplification*, or *Copy of the said Memorials*, and the *Journal of Proceedings* upon them. The *Liberty and Rules of Speech*, to be sure, they can not fai

in, who will be *Wisest* and *Noblest* of each Soveraignty,
for its own Honour and Safety. If any Difference can
arise between those that come from the same Soveraignty
that then One of the Major Number do give the Balls of
that Soveraignty. I should think it extremely necessary,
that every Soveraignty should be present under great
Penalties, and that none leave the Session without Leave,
till *All* be finished ; and that Neutralities in Debates
should by no Means be endured : For any such Latitude
will quickly open a Way to unfair Proceedings, and be
followed by a Train, both of seen, and unseen Inconveniences. I will say little of the *Language* in which the
Session of the Soveraign Estates should be held, but to be
sure it must be in *Latin* or *French* ; the first would be
very well for Civilians, but the last most easie for Men of
Quality.

Sect. IX. *Of the Objections that may be advanced
against the Design.*

I will first give an Answer to the Objections that may
be offered against my *Proposal :* And in my next and
last Section, I shall endeavour to shew some of the mani-
fold Conveniences that would follow this *European
League,* or *Confederacy.*

The first of them is this, *That the strongest and Richest Soveraignty will never agree to it, and if it should,
there would be Danger of Corruption more than of Force
one Time or other.* I answer to the first Part, he is not
stronger than all the rest, and for that Reason you should
promote this, and compel him into it ; especially before
he be so, for then, it will be too late to deal with such an
one. To the last Part of the Objection, I say the Way
is as open now as then ; and it may be the Number fewer,
and as easily come at. However, if Men of Sense and
Honour, and Substance, are chosen, they will either
scorn the Baseness, or have wherewith to pay for the
Knavery : At least they may be watch't so, that one may
be a check upon the other, and all prudently limited by
the Soveraignty they Represent.   In all great Points,
especially before a final Resolve, they may be obliged to
transmit to their Principles, the Merits of such important

Cases depending, and receive their last Instructions: which may be done in four and Twenty Days at the most, as the Place of their Session may be appointed.

The Second is, *That it will endanger an Effeminacy by such a Disuse of the Trade of Soldiery; That if there should be any Need for it, upon any Occasion, we should be at a Loss as they were in* Holland in 72.

There can be no Danger of Effeminacy, because each Soveraignty may introduce as temperate or Severe a Discipline in the Education of Youth, as thev please, by low Living, and due Labour. Instruct them in Mechanical Knowledge, and in Natural Philosophy, by Operation, which is the Honour of the *German* Nobility. This would make them Men: Neither *Women* nor *Lyons*: For *Soldiers* are t'other Extream to Effeminacy. But the Knowledge of Nature, and the useful as well as agreeable Operations of Art, give Men an Understanding of themselves, of the World they are born into, how to be useful and serviceable, both to themselves and others: and how to save and help, not injure or destroy. The Knowledge of Government in General; the particular Constitutions of *Europe;* and above all of his own Country, are very recommending Accomplishments. This fits him for the *Parliament,* and *Council at Home,* and the *Courts of Princes and Services* in the *Imperial States abroad.* At least, he is a good Common-Wealths-Man, and can be useful to the Publick, or retire, as there may be Occasion.

To the other Part of the Objection, *of being at a loss for Soldiery as they were in* Holland *in* 72. The Proposal answers for it itself. One has War no more than the other; and will be as much to seek upon Occasion. Nor is it to be thought that any one will keep up such an Army after such an *Empire* is on Foot, which may hazard the Safety of the rest. However, if it be seen requisit, the Question may be askt, by Order of the Soveraign States, why such an one either raises or keeps up a formidable Body of Troops, and he obliged forthwith to reform or Reduce them; lest any one, by keeping up a great Body of Troops, should surprize a Neighbour. But a small Force in every other Soveraignty, as it is capable or accustomed to maintain, will certainly prevent that Danger, and Vanquish any such Fear.

The Third Objection is, *That there will be great Want of Employment for younger Brothers of Families; and that the Poor must either turn Soldiers or Thieves.* I have answer'd that in my Return to the Second Objection. We shall have the more *Merchants and Husbandmen*, or *Ingenious Naturalists*, if the Government be but any Thing Solicitous of the *Education of their Youth:* Which, next to the present and immediate Happiness of any Country, ought of all Things to be the *Care* and *Skill* of the Government. For such as the Youth of any Country is bred, such is the next Generation, and the Government in good or bad Hands.

I am come now to the last Objection, *That Soveraign Princes and States will hereby become not Soveraign: a Thing they will never endure.* But this also, under Correction, is a Mistake, for they remain as Soveraign at Home as ever they were. Neither their Power over their People, nor the usual Revenue they pay them, is diminished: It may be the War Establishment may be reduced, which will indeed of Course follow, or be better employed to the Advantage of the Publick. So that the *Soveraignties* are as they were, for none of them have now any Soveraignty over one another: And if this be called a lessening of their Power, it must be only because the great Fish can no longer eat up the little ones, and that each Soveraignty is *equally defended* from Injuries, and disabled from committing them: *Cedant Arma Togæ* is a Glorious Sentence; the *Voice of the Dove; the Olive Branch of Peace.* A Blessing so great, that when it pleases God to chastise us severely for our Sins, it is with the *Rod of War* that, for the most Part, he whips us: And Experience tells us none leaves deeper Marks behind it.

Sect. X. *Of the real Benefits that flow from this Proposal about Peace.*

I am come to my last Section, in which I shall enumerate some of those many *real Benefits* that flow from this Proposal, for the Present and Future *Peace* of *Europe.*

Let it not, I pray, be the least, that it prevents the Spilling of so much *Humane and Christian Blood:* For a Thing so offensive to God, and terrible and afflicting to Men, as that has ever been, must recommend our Expedient beyond all Objections. For what can a Man give in Exchange for his Life, as well as Soul? And tho' the chiefest in Government are seldom personally exposed, yet it is a Duty incumbent upon them to be tender of the Lives of their People; since without all Doubt, they are accountable to God for the Blood that is spilt in their Service. So that besides the Loss of so many Lives, of importance to any Government, both for Labour and Propagation, the Cries of so many Widows, Parents and Fatherless are prevented, that cannot be very pleasant in the Ears of any Government, and is the *Natural Consequence of War in all Government.*

There is another *manifest Benefit* which redounds to *Christendom,* by this *Peaceable* Expedient. *The Reputation of Christianity will in some Degree be recovered in the Sight of Infidels;* which, by the many Bloody and unjust *Wars of Christians,* not only with them, but *one* with *another,* hath been greatly impaired. For, to the Scandal of that Holy Profession, *Christians,* that glory in their *Saviour's Name,* have long devoted the Credit and Dignity of it to their worldly Passions, as often as they have been excited by the Impulses of Ambition or Revenge. They have not always been in the Right: Nor has Right been the Reason of *War:* And not only *Christians* against *Christians,* but the same Sort of *Christians* have embrewed *their Hands in one another's Blood:* Invoking and Interesting, all they could, the *Good* and *Merciful God to prosper their Arms to their Brethren's Destruction:* Yet their *Saviour* has told them, *that he came to save, and not to destroy the Lives of Men:* To give and plant *Peace* among Men: And if in any Sense he may be said to send *War,* it is the *Holy War* indeed; for it is to send against the *Devil,* and not the *Persons of Men.* Of all his Titles this seems the most Glorious as well as comfortable for us, that he is the *Prince of Peace.* It is his *Nature,* his *Office,* his *Work,* and the *End,* and excellent Blessings of his Coming, who is both the Maker and Preserver of our *Peace* with God. And it is very remarkable, that in all the *New Testament* he is but once called *Lyon*, but frequently the *Lamb of God;* to denote to us his *Gentle, Meek,* and *Harmless Nature;* and that those who desire to be the *Disciples* of his *Cross and Kingdom,* for they are *inseparable,* must be like him, as St. *Paul,* St. *Peter,* and St. *John,* tell us. Nor is it said the *Lamb* shall lye down with the *Lyon,* but the *Lyon* shall lye down with the *Lamb.* That is *War* shall yield to *Peace,* and the Soldier turn Hermite. To be sure, *Christians* should not be apt to strive, not *swift* to Anger against any Body, and less with one another, and least of all for the uncertain and fading Enjoyments of this Lower World: And no Quality is exempted from this Doctrine. Here is a wide Field for the Reverend Clergy of *Europe* to act their Part in, who have so much the Possession of Princes and People too. May they recommend and labour this pacifick Means I offer, which will end Blood, if not Strife; and then *Reason,* upon free Debate, will be *Judge,* and not the *Sword.* So that both *Right* and *Peace,* which are the Desire and Fruit of wise Governments, and the choice Blessings of any Country, seem to succeed the Establishment of this Proposal.

The third Benefit is, that it saves *Money,* both to the Prince and People; and thereby prevents those Grudgings and Misunderstandings between them that are wont to follow the devouring Expences of *War;* and enables both to perform Publick Acts for *Learning, Charity, Manufactures,* etc. The Virtues of Government and Ornaments of Countries. Nor is this all the *Advantage* that follows to *Soveraignties,* upon this *Head* of Money and good *Husbandry,* to whose Service and Happiness this short Discourse is dedicated; for it saves the great Expence that frequent and splendid Embassies require, and all their Appendages of *Spies and Intelligence,* which in the most prudent Governments, have devoured mighty Sums of Money; and that not without some *immoral Practices also:* Such as *Corrupting of Servants* to betray their *Masters,* by revealing their Secrets; not to be defended by *Christian* or *Old Roman Virtues.* But here, where there is nothing to fear, there is little to know, and therefore the *Purchase* is either *cheap*, or may be wholly *spared*. I might mention *Pensions* to the *Widows* and *Orphans* of such as dye in Wars, and of those that have been *disabled* in them ; which rise high in the Revenue of some Countries.

Our fourth Advantage is, that the *Towns, Cities and Countries, that might be laid waste by the Rage of War, are thereby preserved :* A Blessing that would be very well understood in *Flanders* and *Hungary*, and indeed upon all the *Borders* of *Soveraignties,* which are almost ever the *Stages* of Spoil and Misery ; of which the Stories of *England and Scotland* do sufficiently inform us without looking over the *Water.*

The fifth Benefit of this Peace, is the *Ease and Security of Travel and Traffick :* An Happiness never understood since the *Roman Empire* has been broken into so many *Soveraignties.* But we may easily conceive the Comfort and *Advantage* of travelling through the Governments of *Europe* by a *Pass* from any of the *Soveraignties* of it, which this League and State of *Peace* will *naturally make Authentick:* They that have travel'd *Germany,* where is so great a Number of *Soveraignties,* know the Want and Value of this Privilege, by the many *Stops and Examinations* they meet with by the Way : But especially such as have made the *great Tour of Europe.* This leads to the Benefit of an *Universal Monarchy,* without the Inconveniences that attend it : For when the whole was one *Empire,* tho' these Advantages were enjoyed, yet the several Provinces, that now make the *Kingdoms and States* of *Europe,* were under some Hardship from the great Sums of *Money* remitted to the Imperial Seat, and the Ambition and Avarice of their several *Pro-consuls* and *Governours,* and the great *Taxes* they paid to the *Numerous Legions of Soldiers,* that they maintained for their own Subjection, who were not wont to entertain that Concern for them (being uncertainly there, and having their Fortunes to make) which their respective and proper *Soveraigns* have always shown for them. So that to be *Ruled by Native Princes or States,* with the Advantage of that Peace and Security that can only render an *Universal Monarchy desirable*, is peculiar to our Proposal, and for that Reason it is to be preferred.

Another Advantage is, *The Great Security it will be to Christians against the Inroads of the* Turk, *in their most Prosperous Fortune.* For it had been impossible for the *Port,* to have prevailed so often, and so far from *Christendom,* but by the Carelessness, or Wilful Connivence, if not Aid, of some *Christian Princes.* And for the same Reason, why no *Christian Monarch* will adventure to oppose, or break such an Union, the *Grand Seignior* will find himself obliged to concur, for the Security of what he holds in *Europe:* Where, with all his Strength, he would feel it an Over-Match for him. *The Prayers, Tears, Treason, Blood and Devastation, that War has cost in* Christendom, *for these Two last Ages especially, must add to the Credit of our Proposal, and the Blessing of the* Peace *thereby humbly recommended.*

The Seventh Advantage of an *European, Imperial Dyet, Parliament,* or *Estates, is, That it will beget and increase Personal Friendship between Princes and States,* which tends to the Rooting up of Wars, and Planting Peace in a Deep and Fruitful Soil. For Princes have the Curiosity of seeing the Courts and Cities of other Countries, as well as Private Men, if they could as securely and familiarly gratify their Inclinations. It were a great Motive to the Tranquility of the World, *That they could freely Converse Face to Face, and Personally and Reciprocally Give and Receive Marks of Civility and Kindness.* An *Hospitality* that leaves these Impressions behind it, will hardly let Ordinary Matters prevail, to Mistake or Quarrel one another. Their *Emulation would be in the Instances of Goodness, Laws, Customs, Learning, Arts, Buildings;* and in particular those that relate to *Charity,* the True Glory of some Governments, where Beggars are as much a Rarity, as in other Places it would be to see none.

Nor is this all the Benefit that would come by this *Freedom* and *Interview of Princes:* For *Natural Affection* would hereby be preserved, which we see little better than lost, *from the Time their Children,* or *Sisters, are Married into Other Courts.* For the present State and Insincerity of Princes forbid them the Enjoyment of that Natural Comfort which is possest by Private Families: Insomuch,

that from the Time a Daughter, or Sister is Married to
another Crown, Nature is submitted to Interest, and that,
for the most Part, grounded not upon Solid or Commendable Foundations, but *Ambition*, or *Unjust Avarice.* I
say, this Freedom, that is the Effect of our Pacifick Pro_
posal, restores *Nature* to Her Just Right and Dignity in
the Families of Princes, and them to the Comfort She
brings, wherever She is preserved in Her proper Station.
Here *Daughters* may Personally intreat their *Parents*, and
Sisters their *Brothers*, for a good Understanding between
them and their *Husbands*, where Nature, not crush'd by
Absence, and Sinister Interests, but acting by the Sight
and Lively Entreaties of such near Relations, is almost
sure to prevail.   They cannot easily resist the most
affectionate Addresses of such powerful Solicitors, *as
their Children, and Grand-Children*, and their *Sisters,
Nephews*, and *Nieces:* And so backward from *Children
to Parents*, and *Sisters to Brothers*, to keep up and preserve their own Families, by a good Understanding between their Husbands and them.

To conclude this Section, there is yet another Manifest
Privilege that follows this *Intercourse* and Good Understanding, which methinks should be very moving with
Princes, viz. *That hereby they may chuse Wives for themselves*, such as they Love, and not by *Proxy* meerly to
gratify Interest; an ignoble Motive; and that rarely be-
gets, or continues that *Kindness* which ought to be between Men and their Wives.   A Satisfaction very few
Princes ever knew, and to which all other Pleasures
ought to resign.   Which has often obliged me to think.
*That the Advantage of Private Men upon Princes, by
Family Comforts, is a sufficient Ballance against their
Greater Power and Glory: The one being more in* Imagination, *than* Real; *and often* Unlawful; *but the other*,
Natural, Solid, *and* Commendable.   Besides, it is certain, Parents Loving Well before they are Married, which
very rarely happens to Princes, *has Kind and Generous
Influences upon their Offspring: Which, with their Ex-
ample, makes them better Husbands, and Wives, in their
Turn.*   This, in great Measure, prevents Unlawful Love,
and the Mischiefs of those Intriegues that are wont to

follow them: What *Hatred*, *Feuds*, *Wars*, *and Desola-*
tions have, in divers Ages, flown from Unkindness between
Princes and their Wives? What *Unnatural Divisions*
among their Children, and Ruin to their Families, if not
Loss of their Countries by it? Behold an Expedient to prevent it, a Natural and Efficacious One : Happy to Princes,
and Happy to their People also. For Nature being renewed
and strengthened by these Mutual Pledges and Endear-
ments, I have mentioned, will leave those soft and kind Impressions behind in the Minds of Princes that *Court and*
Country will very easily discern and feel the Good Effects
of : Especially if they have the Wisdom to show that they
Interest themselves in the Prosperity of the Children and
Relations of their Princes. For it does not only incline
them to be Good, but engage those Relations to become
Powerful Suitors to their Princes for them, if any Misun-
derstanding should unhappily arise between them and their
Soveraigns : Thus ends this *Section.* It now rests to conclude the Discourse, in which, if I have not pleased my
Reader, or answered his Expectation, it is some Comfort
to me I meant well, and have cost him but little Money
and Time ; and Brevity is an Excuse, if not a Virtue,
where the Subject is not agreeable, or is but ill prose-
cuted.

THE CONCLUSION.

I Will conclude this *my Proposal of an European, Sov-*
eraign, or *Imperial Dyet*, *Parliament*, or *Estates*, with
that which I have touch'd upon before, and which falls
under the Notice of every One concerned, by coming
Home to their Particular and Respective Experience
within their own *Soveraignties.* That by the same *Rules*
of Justice and Prudence, by which Parents and Masters
Govern their Families, and Magistrates their Cities, and
Estates their Republicks, and Princes and Kings their
Principalities and Kingdoms, *Europe* may obtain and Preserve *Peace among Her Soveraignties.* For Wars are the
Duels of Princes ; and as Government in Kingdoms and
States, *Prevents Men being Judges and Executioners for*
themselves, over-rules Private Passions as to Injuries or
Revenge, and subjects the Great as well as the Small to
the *Rule of Justice*, that Power might not vanquish or

oppress Right, nor one Neighbour act an *Independency and Soveraignty upon another*, while they have resigned that Original Claim to the Benefit and Comfort of Society; so this being soberly weighed in the Whole, and Parts of it, it will not be hard to conceive or frame, nor yet to execute the Design I have here proposed.

And for the better understanding and perfecting of the *Idea*, I here present to the *Soveraign Princes and Estates of Europe*, for the Safety and Tranquility of it, I must recommend to their Perusals *Sir William Temple's Account of the United Provinces;* which is an Instance and Answer, upon *Practice*, to all the Objections that can be advanced against the Practicability of my Proposal : Nay, it is an Experiment that not only comes to our Case, but exceeds the Difficulties that can render its Accomplishment disputable. For there we shall find *Three Degrees of Soveraignties to make up every Soveraignty in the General States.* I will reckon them backwards : First, *The States General themselves;* then the *Immediate Soveraignties* that Constitute them, which are those of the *Provinces*, answerable to the *Soveraignties of Europe*, that by their *Deputies* are to compose the *European Dyet*, *Parliament* or *Estates* in our Proposal : And then there are the several Cities of each *Province*, that are so many *Independent* or *Distinct Soveraignties*, which compose those of the *Provinces*, as those of the *Provinces* do compose the *States General* at the *Hague.*

But I confess I have the Passion to wish heartily, that the Honour of Proposing and Effecting so Great and Good a Design, might be owing to *England*, of all the Countries in *Europe*, as something of the Nature of our Expedient was, in Design and Preparation, to the Wisdom, Justice, and Valour, *of Henry the Fourth of France*, whose Superior Qualities raising his Character above those of His Ancestors, or Contemporaries, deservedly gave Him the Stile of *Henry the Great*. For *He was upon obliging the Princes and Estates of Europe to a Political Ballance*, when the *Spanish Faction*, for that Reason, contrived, and accomplished *His Murder*, by the Hands of *Ravilliac*. I will not then fear to be censured, for proposing an *Expedient* for the Present and Future *Peace of Europe*, when it was not only the *Design*, *but Glory of One of the Greatest Princes that ever reigned in it;* and is found Practicable in the Constitution of one of the Wisest and Powerfullest States of it. So that to conclude, I have very Little to answer for in all this Affair ; because, if it succeed, I have so Little to deserve : For this *Great King's Example tells us it is fit to be done;* and Sir *William Temple's History* shews us, by a Surpassing Instance, *That it may be done;* and *Europe*, by her Incomparable Miseries, makes it now *Necessary to be done :* That my Share is only thinking of it at this Juncture, and putting it into the Common Light for the Peace and Prosperity of *Europe*.